Vivaldi,
Of Course!

Vivaldi, Of Course!

Provocative and Challenging Quizzes for Overeducated, Really Smart People Who Have Nothing Better to Do

Danny Gurr

BARNES
& NOBLE
BOOKS

NEW YORK

Contents

Introduction

Despite its relatively modest size, the book you are holding was more than twenty-five years in the making. As a lifelong reader of history and reference books, I have always collected odds and ends of (sometimes) useful information. *Vivaldi, Of Course!* represents the tip of the iceberg of this vast collection. It is a book that is designed to both challenge your knowledge across a wide range of subjects and to pique your interest in learning more about those subjects with which you are not very familiar.

You will enjoy this book if you like testing both your memory as well as your power of deductive reasoning. Although many of the quizzes consist of multiple-choice questions, more than one of the potential answers should usually appear plausible. My goal is to pose questions that provide just enough information to require the reader to produce a bit of "mental perspiration." Even if some questions appear easy at first glance, I hope you will occasionally have to pause and reflect in order to arrive at the correct answer.

In the vast majority of cases you may already have a working knowledge of the subject area. You will probably find that you learned it years ago at school, work or even from a cable television show. Much of it is important, useful knowledge. In fact, it would trivialize this valuable information to call it trivia! If you are at all like me, you will find some small satisfaction in knowing that you still grasp the basic principles of such things as Euclidean geometry, even if it has been a while since you had to think about them.

Several of my brilliant and helpful friends (you know who you are) were kind enough to submit to taking some of the quizzes in this book. It is always interesting to see how they respond both when they answer a question correctly and, even more so, when they answer incorrectly.

The least interesting response is when they immediately know the correct answer. With few exceptions, a quick correct answer elicits the statement, "That was easy." Of course, what is considered "easy" varies from individual to individual. However, my informal survey reveals a curious pattern. If an individual believes himself to be adept at a particular subject, then he tends to think that the quiz is easy and that only a few of the questions were challenging. The same quiz, when given to another talented person who does not feel as adept at the subject, is invariably described as being difficult with only a few easy questions. This is true even if both individuals answer the same number of questions correctly.

An incorrect answer can actually be much more fun than a correct response. Without a doubt, a wrong answer can provide grist for discussion and debate. If I have failed to pose a question with enough information to make anything more than a guess possible, or if the intended clues are simply too obscure, then the question can still be your springboard to further investigation. In my case it never fails that, when I dip into an almanac, encyclopedia or atlas looking for one specific fact, I always end up lingering for hours making unintended discoveries. Hopefully, the questions in *Vivaldi, Of Course!* that stump you will point you in the direction of buried treasures of new information.

The third possible response, as suggested by the title, *Vivaldi, Of Course!*, is the frustrating case where the correct answer is almost within your grasp but just manages to elude you. No doubt, as you work your way through these quizzes, you will say to yourself, "I should have known that one!" or "I can't believe I missed this one!" The frequency of your frustration will likely depend upon the time constraints you put upon yourself to complete each quiz. So take your time and let the quiz prompt your discovery (or rediscovery) of something of interest. Personally, I am stubborn enough to ruminate for days on the solution to a challenging question. If I think the answer may lie buried in the back of my mind, then I like to take the time to dig it up!

A large part of the fun of this collection of quizzes is that it should present a number of challenges to almost anyone. Sports fans will inevitably ace the sports quiz but will hopefully find many other subjects more difficult. Movie buffs will likely not have any trouble with the Hollywood quiz, but perhaps geography or mathematics will present a challenge. To do well with the quizzes in this book it would be helpful to possess a river of general knowledge that is a mile wide and at least a few inches deep.

Finally, if you like *Vivaldi, Of Course!* I encourage you to look for more books from Black Dog & Leventhal Publishers. Mr. Leventhal is, himself, a Renaissance man of great wit and enormous knowledge. His eclectic catalog of clever books always delights his many friends and fans, of whom I am very happy to include myself.

So now, let the games begin!

American History

1. All or part of which six states were created by the Northwest Territory Act of 1787?

2. What southern city was named after King George III's wife who was from Mecklenburg-Strelitz?

3. What state was previously named "Franklin" in honor of Benjamin Franklin?

   a) Alabama
   b) Kentucky
   c) Ohio
   d) Tennessee

4. Match the state with the year of its first permanent European settlement:

A. Delaware	1. 1607
B. Georgia	2. 1620
C. Maryland	3. 1623
D. Massachusetts	4. 1624
E. New Hampshire	5. 1634
F. New York	6. 1636
G. Virginia	7. 1638
H. Rhode Island	8. 1670
I. South Carolina	9. 1733

5. In what year did Colorado become a state?

6. The Louisiana Purchase of 1803 added over 900,000 square miles to the United States. All or part of which thirteen states were created from this territory?

7. Young Benjamin Franklin worked in his father Josiah's shop. What was Josiah's business?

   a) Bookseller   c) Chandler
   b) Printer   d) Blacksmith

8. The deadly duel between Alexander Hamilton and Aaron Burr took place in New Jersey because dueling was illegal in New York, where they both lived. What city was the site of the 1804 duel?

   a) Bayonne   c) Hoboken
   b) Fort Lee   d) Weehawken

9. Which of these Virginians did not serve in the First Continental Congress?

   a) Patrick Henry   c) Edmund Pendleton
   b) Thomas Jefferson   d) George Washington

10. In addition to Thomas Jefferson, who were the other four men who formed the committee to draft the Declaration of Independence?

11. Who nominated George Washington to serve as commander of the Continental Army?

a) John Adams   c) John Hancock

b) Benjamin Franklin   d) Thomas Jefferson

12. Who was the first person to resign as vice president of the United States?

a) Aaron Burr   c) Henry Clay

b) John C. Calhoun   d) Spiro Agnew

13. Elected at age 36, who was the youngest vice president of the United States?

a) John Quincy Adams

b) John Breckinridge

c) Aaron Burr

d) Theodore Roosevelt

14. What is the date of each of these significant events in American history?

A. Columbus's discovery of the New World?

B. Pilgrims landing at Plymouth?

C. Battles of Lexington and Concord?

D. Surrender of Cornwallis at Yorktown?

E. Jackson's victory at the Battle of New Orleans?

F. Evacuation of Fort Sumter?

G. Lee's surrender at Appomattox?

H. End of World War I?

I. Great stock market crash?

J. Attack on Pearl Harbor?

K. Assassination of JFK?

L. Neil Armstrong's moon walk?

15. Which of Robert E. Lee's former cavalry generals founded the Ku Klux Klan in Pulaski, Tennessee?

a) Pierre Beauregard
b) Nathan Bedford Forrest
c) Thomas "Stonewall" Jackson
d) J. E. B. Stuart

16. What member of Congress from Montana voted against U.S. entry into both world wars?

17. Which Native American tribe, led by Chief Massasoit, was friendly to the original Plymouth pilgrims?

a) Narragansetts
b) Nipmucks
c) Pequots
d) Wampanoags

18. One of the earliest efforts by a Native American to lead a united tribal alliance against European settlers was led by which chief of the Ottawa tribe?

a) Metacom
b) Pontiac
c) Tecumseh
d) Tippecanoe

19. Which of these was not one of the tribes in the Iroquois of Five Nations league?

a) Huron
b) Mohawk
c) Oneida
d) Onondaga

20. Which European country is the origin for the largest number of U.S. citizens?

a) England
b) Germany
c) Ireland
d) Italy

The American Revolution

$1.$ "The Battle of Bunker Hill" took place largely on which other nearby hill?

   a) Breed's Hill   c) Beacon Hill

   b) Copp's Hill   d) Babson's Hill

$2.$ How many people were killed at the Boston Massacre?

   a) 18   c) 5

   b) 12   d) 2

$3.$ Which one of the thirteen original colonies did not send a representative to the First Continental Congress?

   a) Georgia   c) New Hampshire

   b) South Carolina   d) New York

$4.$ General William Howe withdrew his troops from Boston when faced with likely defeat due to:

   a) The arrival of French troops from Quebec.

   b) The activation of local militia following Paul Revere's ride.

   c) Captured artillery installed on Dorchester Heights.

   d) The impending arrival of the French fleet in Boston Harbor.

5. Match the date with the event:

A.	March 1765	1.	British General Howe withdraws from Boston
B.	March 1770	2.	Parliament passes the Stamp Act
C.	December 1773	3.	Boston Tea Party
D.	September 1774	4.	First Continental Congress opens in Philadelphia
E.	April 1775	5.	Boston Massacre
F.	June 1775	6.	Battle of Bunker Hill
G.	March 1776	7.	British march on Lexington and Concord
H.	July 1776	8.	Declaration of Independence is adopted by Congress

6. The resolution on independence was proposed to Congress by which Virginian?

a) Patrick Henry   c) Thomas Jefferson
b) Richard Lee   d) George Washington

7. Which two states voted "No" in the initial vote on the resolution on independence?

8. Following the Treaty of Alliance, 5,500 troops under the Comte de Rochambeau arrived in America to support Washington's Continental Army. Where did the French troops land and establish their initial headquarters?

a) Long Island, NY   c) Portsmouth, NH
b) Newport, RI   d) Charleston, SC

9. Benedict Arnold was commander of what fort when he betrayed the American cause?

    a) West Point   c) Ticonderoga
    b) Saratoga   d) McHenry

10. What British agent, while serving as Benedict Arnold's accomplice, was captured by Washington's troops and hung as an enemy spy?

    a) George Frobisher   c) William Grafton
    b) Paul Wentworth   d) John Andre

11. Who was nicknamed the "Swampfox" of the revolution as a result of his elusive tactics in South Carolina?

    a) Banastre Tarleton   c) Henry Laurens
    b) Francis Marion   d) Daniel Morgan

12. Which single event most influenced the French decision to support the American cause?

    a) British loss at the Battle of Saratoga
    b) Diplomatic efforts of Thomas Jefferson in Paris
    c) Opportunity to reclaim Canada from a defeated Britain
    d) Propaganda sent back to France by Lafayette

13. Which of these men was not a delegate to the Paris peace commission that negotiated the treaty officially ending the war in September, 1783?

    a) Benjamin Franklin   c) John Jay
    b) John Adams   d) Silas Deane

14. Approximately how many American soldiers are estimated to have died during the Revolutionary War?

    a) 25,000   c) 125,000
    b) 75,000   d) 200,000

15. Over the course of the war it is estimated that over 100,000 loyal Tories left the United States. Many of them were rewarded with land grants in what British-controlled territory?

a) Ireland
b) Nova Scotia
c) Australia
d) Bermuda

16. Caron de Beaumarchais was instrumental in securing French financial support for the American cause. This somewhat unusual character is best remembered as a:

a) Scientist
b) Balloonist
c) Playwright
d) Painter

17. Which of these towns did not serve as headquarters for Congress during the Revolutionary War?

a) Baltimore, MD
b) Lancaster, PA
c) Plymouth, MA
d) York, PA

18. What man was the president of the First Continental Congress?

a) John Hancock
b) Patrick Henry
c) Henry Laurens
d) Peyton Randolph

19. True or false? George Washington never permitted African-American troops to serve in the Continental Army, although a few served for brief periods in the Pennsylvania militia as substitutes for pacifist Quakers.

20. Washington believed that a conspiracy later called the Conway Cabal intended to replace him as commander in chief with which general?

a) Nathanael Greene
b) Horatio Gates
c) Anthony Wayne
d) Charles Lee

Ancient History and Civilizations

1. The Great Pyramids lie in which direction from the Nile?

   a) North   c) South
   b) East   d) West

2. At 481 feet, the Great Pyramid of King Khufu was the tallest structure ever constructed until which of the following was completed in 1889?

   a) Big Ben   c) Eiffel Tower
   b) Washington Monument   d) U.S. Capitol Dome

3. Name the Seven Wonders of the World.

4. Approximately how old was King Tutankhamen when he came to the throne in Egypt?

   a) 9   c) 17
   b) 13   d) 20

5. Who led the team that discovered King Tut's tomb in the Valley of the Kings in 1922?

   a) Carter James   c) James Howard
   b) Howard Carter   d) Howard James

6. Approximately how many different hieroglyphic symbols have been identified?

a) 50
b) 200
c) 700
d) 1800

7. Three languages appear on the famous Rosetta stone, which was discovered in 1799. Which of the languages below does not appear on the stone?

a) Greek
b) Demotic
c) Hieroglyphs
d) Persian

8. What was Cleopatra's first language?

a) Greek
b) Persian
c) Arabic
d) Latin

9. Greek cultures developed on many of the islands of the Aegean. One of the oldest and greatest was the Minoan, which was centered on which island?

a) Rhodes
b) Cyprus
c) Lesbos
d) Crete

10. The golden age of Athens, marked by the age of Pericles, occurred during which of these time periods?

a) Second century B.C.
b) Third century B.C.
c) Fourth century B.C.
d) Fifth century B.C.

11. Which city-state won the Peloponnesian War?

a) Sparta
b) Thebes
c) Athens
d) Troy

12. Pericles was one of Athens' ten elected military commanders. What were these elite officials called?

a) Centurions   c) Decadians

b) Senators   d) Strategos

13. What was the outcome of the historic Battle of Marathon?

a) Athenians beat the Spartans

b) Greeks lost to the Romans

c) Greeks beat the Persians

d) Spartans beat the Athenians

14. Which Persian king led his forces at the critical naval battle of Salamis?

a) Xerxes   c) Saladin

b) Darius   d) Hamurabi

15. Put these philosophers in chronological order:

A. Diogenes   C. Plato

B. Aristotle   D. Socrates

16. Match the famous Greek with his profession:

A. Hippocrates	1. Poet
B. Pythagoras	2. Biographer
C. Heredotus	3. Playwright
D. Phidias	4. Physician
E. Solon	5. Historian
F. Aeschylus	6. Orator
G. Demosthenes	7. Mathematician
H. Epicurus	8. Legislator
I. Homer	9. Sculptor
J. Plutarch	10. Philosopher

17. How many infantry soldiers would be included in a typical Roman legion?

a) 100   c) 1,000

b) 500   d) 5,000

18. Match the Roman province with the modern nation in which it would be contained:

A. Mauretania   1. Croatia

B. Gaul   2. Bulgaria

C. Dalmatia   3. Morocco

D. Lusitania   4. Romania

E. Thrace   5. France

F. Dacia   6. Portugal

19. Put these Romans in chronological order:

A. Augustus

B. Julius Caesar

C. Caligula

D. Tiberius

E. Nero

F. Claudius

20. Who was the leader of the tribe that sacked Rome in 410?

a) Attila   c) Barbarosa

b) Ivan   d) Alaric

Animal
Kingdom

1. Approximately how many bird species currently exist?

    a) 2,000   c) 6,000
    b) 4,000   d) 9,000

2. The fossil of which feathered creature from the Jurassic period was discovered in Germany in 1861?

    a) Ovipositor   c) Aepyornis
    b) Areosaurus   d) Archaeopteryx

3. The large, flightless dodo bird, which became extinct in the late seventeenth century, was found on what island?

    a) Mauritius   c) Java
    b) Australia   d) New Guinea

4. The smallest species of bird, the bee hummingbird, typically weighs how much?

    a) .05 oz.   c) 1.5 oz.
    b) 0.5 oz.   d) 5.0 oz.

5. True or false? Despite their small size, some hummingbirds annually migrate hundreds of miles.

6. Chimpanzees are usually classified as the most intelligent animal. How similar is their genetic makeup to that of humans?

a) 68%   c) 88%
b) 78%   d) 98%

7. There are four species of great apes. Which of these is not one of them?

a) Chimpanzee   c) Orangutan
b) Baboon   d) Bonobo

8. There are as many species of fish as there are birds, reptiles and mammals combined. How many species of fish exist?

a) 2,000   c) 50,000
b) 20,000   d) 250,000

9. A North American lobster can grow to more than 40 lb. and live up to how many years?

a) 10   c) 50
b) 20   d) 100

10. Salmon are a species that live in salt water but migrate to fresh water to spawn. This trait is known as:

a) Catadromous   c) Salatinous
b) Anadromous   d) Monotrymous

11. Which of the following are fish?

A. Narwhal   F. Manta
B. Sea horse   G. Squid
C. Starfish   H. Lamprey
D. Jellyfish   I. Skate
E. Eel   J. Whale shark

12. Match the order of mammals with the member of its species:

A. Carnivores   1. Moles
B. Even-toed hooves   2. Beavers
C. Insectivores   3. Pandas
D. Marsupials   4. Tamarins
E. Monotremes   5. Pigs
F. Odd-toed hooves   6. Possums
G. Primates   7. Armadillos
H. Rodents   8. Horses
I. Edentates   9. Echidnas
J. Pangolins   10. Scaly anteater

13. The first mammals appeared 230 million years ago during which period?

a) Triassic   c) Cambrian
b) Jurassic   d) Cretaceous

14. Which of these species of mammals lays eggs?

a) Echidnas   c) Armadillos
b) Aardvarks   d) Scaly anteaters

15. Which of these is not a reptile:

a) Turtle   c) Salamander
b) Skink   d) Chameleon

16. Which one of these four orders of reptiles includes two species that look very similar to lizards?

a) Tuataras   c) Serpents

b) Caecilians   d) Newts

17. There are approximately _____ species of insects known to exist.

a) 250,000   c) 2,000,000

b) 900,000   d) 4,500,000

18. Which of the following are insects?

A. Scorpions

B. Spiders

C. Crabs

D. Fleas

E. Beetles

F. Spiders

G. Ticks

H. Centipedes

I. Shrimp

J. Butterflies

19. The largest insect societies can contain up to 5 million of which insect?

a) Termites   c) Wasps

b) Ants   d) Bees

20. Which of these snakes is not poisonous?

a) African Cape cobra   c) African black mamba

b) Indian python   d) Asian krait

Architecture

1. Match the skyscraper with its city:

A. Petronas Towers	1. Chicago
B. Aon Center	2. Dubai
C. Jin Mao Building	3. Hong Kong
D. Central Plaza	4. New York
E. Emirates Towers	5. Shanghai
F. Woolworth Building	6. Yokohama
G. Baiyoke Tower	7. Kuala Lumpur
H. Landmark Tower	8. Bangkok

2. New York and Chicago are famous for their skyscrapers, but four other U.S. cities have at least one building that is over 1,000 feet tall. Name these four cities.

3. What city boasts the world's largest capacity sports stadium?

   a) New Orleans   c) Sao Paulo
   b) Prague   d) Sydney

4. Name the rectangular pilaster formed by thickening the end of a wall.

   a) Anta   c) Column
   b) Buttress   d) Entablature

5. Three of America's largest suspension bridges are in New York. Which of these is not among the nation's ten largest?

a) Brooklyn Bridge
b) Bronx-Whitestone Bridge
c) George Washington Bridge
d) Verrazano-Narrows Bridge

6. What bridge ranks fifth among U.S. suspension bridges at 2,800 feet long?

a) Delaware Memorial Bridge
b) Golden Gate Bridge
c) San Francisco-Oakland Bay Bridge
d) Tacoma Narrows Bridge

7. What country boasts the largest suspension bridge at 6,529 feet long?

a) China   c) Korea
b) Japan   d) Malaysia

8. Who designed the beautiful Mosque of Suleiman in Constantinople during the Ottoman Empire?

a) Churriguera   c) Shawwal
b) Mehmed   d) Sinan

9. Which architect drew the original design for Saint Peter's cathedral in Rome in 1506?

a) Alberti   c) Guarini
b) Bramante   d) Piranesi

10. Which architect introduced the Palladian style to London?

a) Capability Brown   c) Thomas Hamilton
b) Inigo Jones   d) William Butterfield

11. Which architect is famous for the Regency style in London during the early nineteenth century?

a) Kent   c) Soane

b) Nash   d) Wren

12. Match the classical order with its description:

A. Doric   1. Plain column, simple base, ornate capital

B. Ionic   2. Fluted column, no base, simple capital

C. Corinthian   3. Fluted column, simple base, scroll capital

13. What architectural style is defined by pointed arches and ribbed vaulting?

14. Which of these is not a common type of arched-roof vault?

a) Barrel   c) Groin

b) Fan   d) Plinth

15. Which architect, painter and town planner was famous for his development of the International Style?

a) Latrobe   c) Loos

b) Le Corbusier   d) Wright

16. Name the founder of the Bauhaus movement.

a) Gropius   c) Meier

b) Kahn   d) Mies van der Rohe

17. Name the city in which the Bauhaus movement began.

a) Berlin   c) Paris

b) Cologne   d) Weimar

18. Where was Frank Lloyd Wright, founder of the Prairie School, born?

a) Illinois   c) Nebraska
b) Minnesota   d) Wisconsin

19. The Pompidou Center, famous for locating many of its engineering and "service" elements on the outside, was designed by Renzo Piano and whom?

a) Richard Rogers   c) Frank Gehry
b) Norman Foster   d) Philip Johnson

20. Match the architect with his notable building:

A. Charles Barry   1. Guggenheim Bilbao
B. Antonio Gaudi   2. U.S. Capitol Building
C. Frank Gehry   3. Chicago Stock Exchange
D. Cass Gilbert   4. Woolworth Building
E. Walter Gropius   5. Getty Center
F. Philip Johnson   6. Boston Public Library
G. Benjamin Latrobe   7. Seagram Building
H. Richard Meier   8. John Hancock Building, Boston

I. Cesar Pelli   9. Pan Am Building
J. Louis Sullivan   10. Houses of Parliament
K. Stanford White   11. Church of the Holy Family
L. I. M. Pei   12. Petronas Towers

Art History

1. Name the great Florentine painter famous for both *Primavera* and *The Birth of Venus.*

   a) Alberti   c) Fra Angelico
   b) Botticelli d) Masaccio

2. Which of these cities was not a center of painting during the Renaissance?

   a) Ferrara   c) Florence
   b) Flanders   d) Paris

3. Which of these painters is not associated with the Venetian tradition?

   a) Titian   c) Veronese
   b) Tinoretto d) da Vinci

4. Which of these works was not painted by Leonardo da Vinci?

   a) *Annunciation*   c) *Flight Into Egypt*
   b) *Cecilia Gallarani*   d) *Madonna and Saint Anne*

5. How many years did it take Michelangelo to paint the ceiling of the Sistine Chapel?

   a) 4   c) 8
   b) 6   d) 12

6. Whom did Pope Julius II employ to decorate the Vatican apartments?

   a) Bramante

   b) Michelangelo

   c) Raphael

   d) Titian

7. Put these artistic movements in chronological order:

   A. Rococo
   B. Mannerism
   C. Renaissance
   D. Baroque
   E. Pre-Raphaelite
   F. Fauvism
   G. Impressionism

8. Name the great painter in the Mannerist tradition whose works include *Laocoon*, *The Resurrection* and *View of Toledo*.

9. Name the French painter of the Rococo period known for his works *The Swing* and *A Young Girl Reading*.

10. Which of these painters is not typically included among the Hudson River school?

    a) Thomas Cole

    b) Samuel Coleman

    c) Asher Durand

    d) Edward Hopper

11. Which of these English painters was a founder of the Pre-Raphaelite Brotherhood?

    a) Thomas Gainsborough
    b) Sir John Everett Millais
    c) Sir Joshua Reynolds
    d) J. M. W. Turner

12.
Name the influential Parisian painter of the 1860s and 1870s whose works include *The Spanish Singer* and *The Bar at the Folies-Bergere.*

a) Daumier   c) Manet
b) Degas   d) Toulouse-Lautrec

13.
Which American portrait artist painted each of the first five U.S. presidents?

a) Copley   c) Stuart
b) Peale   d) West

14.
Which Connecticut-born painter followed the suggestion of Thomas Jefferson by painting a series of historic American events that included *The Declaration of Independence in Congress, The Surrender of Cornwallis at Yorktown* and *The Battle of Bunker Hill?*

15.
In what year was the term "Impressionists" applied to the group of artists who had exhibited their work at the Salon des Refuses?

a) 1869   c) 1879
b) 1874   d) 1884

16.
Which of the following artists are generally included among the Impressionists?

A. Manet   F. Cassatt
B. Monet   G. Renoir
C. Pissaro   H. Gauguin
D. Poussin   I. Van Gogh
E. Sisley   J. Cézanne

17. Name the master of "pointillism" whose tragically short life limited his repertoire to a few great works including *The Circus, The Lighthouse at Honfleur* and *La Grand Jatte.*

18. What expatriate American painter whose most famous work is properly known as *Arrangement in Grey and Black* sued the English critic John Ruskin over an unkind review?

19. Which of these painters would not be included in a show of "surrealism"?

a) Dali   c) Klee

b) Ernst   d) Magritte

20. Match the artist to the famous work:

A. Hieronymus Bosch	1. *Persistence of Memory*
B. Pieter Brueghel	2. *Dancer at the Bar*
C. Pierre Bonnard	3. *The Kiss*
D. Salvador Dalí	4. *Nighthawks*
E. Edgar Degas	5. *Blue Boy*
F. Paul Gauguin	6. *Guernica*
G. Thomas Gainsborough	7. *Breezing Up*
H. Winslow Homer	8. *Garden of Earthly Delights*
I. Edward Hopper	9. *Sunflowers*
J. Gustav Klimt	10. *Bathers at Tahiti*
K. Henri Matisse	11. *Black Iris*
L. Claude Monet	12. *Peasant Wedding*
M. Georgia O'Keefe	13. *Woman in Black Stockings*
N. Pablo Picasso	14. *Waterlilies*
O. Vincent van Gogh	15. *The Yellow Curtain*

The Bible

1. How many Old Testament books are there in the King James version of the Bible?

    a) 39   c) 43
    b) 41   d) 45

2. Put the first five books of the Bible in the correct order:

    A. Leviticus
    B. Exodus
    C. Deuteronomy
    D. Genesis
    E. Numbers

3. In the fourteenth century, which Oxford theologian produced the first English translation of the Bible?

    a) John Wesley   c) John Wyclif
    b) Thomas Moore   d) William Tyndale

4. How many books are in the New Testament?

    a) 27   c) 31
    b) 29   d) 33

5. What is the name of the Greek translation of the Hebrew Bible that was used until the fourth century?

a) The Apocrypha   c) The Scriptures
b) The Vulgate   d) The Septuagint

6. Which saint translated the Bible from Greek to Latin?

a) Saint John   c) Saint Thomas
b) Saint Thaddeus   d) Saint Jerome

7. Which of these books is included in the main body of the Catholic Old Testament but is not included in the main body of Protestant editions?

a) Judith   c) Esther
b) Ruth   d) Haggai

8. In the King James Bible, what is the sixth commandment?

a) Remember the Sabbath day.
b) Thou shalt not kill.
c) Thou shalt not steal.
d) Thou shalt not commit adultery.

9. In which book of the Bible does the story of the ark and the flood appear?

a) Genesis   c) Psalms
b) Exodus   d) Judges

10. How many sons did Jacob have?

a) 10   c) 12
b) 11   d) 13

11. The kingdom of Assyria conquered Israel in 722 B.C. What was the name of the Assyrian capital that was located on the Tigris River?

 a) Babylon   c) Ur
 b) Nineveh   d) Nimrud

12. Name the king of the Babylonian empire that destroyed Jerusalem in 586 B.C.

 a) Nebuchadnezzar   c) Shalmaneser
 b) Ishtar   d) Hammurabi

13. Who was Jezebel's husband?

 a) Hezekiah   c) Jehu
 b) Ahab   d) Issachar

14. Which of these was not one of Jacob's sons?

 a) Reuben   c) Dan
 b) Levi   d) Esau

15. Put these Old Testament leaders in chronological order:

 A. Jacob
 B. Moses
 C. Saul
 D. Noah
 E. Abraham
 F. Solomon
 G. David
 H. Isaac
 I. Joseph
 J. Joshua

16. Goliath was the champion of what army?

a) Babylonian   c) Phoenician
b) Assyrian   d) Philistine

17. What was the name of Cain and Abel's younger brother?

18. After killing his brother Abel, Cain went east of Eden into which land?

a) Canaan   c) Gomorrah
b) Palestine   d) Nod

19. Which of these apostles was a tax collector?

a) Thomas   c) James
b) Matthew   d) Judas

20. Which of the apostles was Simon Peter's brother?

a) John   c) Philip
b) James   d) Andrew

Business

1. In what year did a bomb explode at the corner of Wall Street and Broad Street, causing the deaths of forty people in New York's financial district?

   a) 1920   c) 1941
   b) 1929   d) 1969

2. Prior to the 1929 stock market crash the Dow Jones Average peaked at 381. In what year did the Dow Jones next close above its pre-crash peak?

   a) 1932   c) 1945
   b) 1941   d) 1954

3. Who did FDR appoint as the first chairman of the SEC?

   a) William O. Douglas   c) James Landis
   b) Joseph Kennedy   d) Dick Whitney

4. What native of Green Cove Springs, FL, was the first successful proponent of the concept of making investing a part of "Main Street" America?

   a) William Barney   c) Charles Merrill
   b) E. F. Hutton   d) Charles Schwab

5. How many stocks are currently used to calculate the Dow Jones Average?

6. Which of these companies was not organized by J. P. Morgan?

a) General Electric
b) International Harvester
c) U.S. Steel
d) Bank of America

7. Which captain of industry served, at different points in time, as president of Carnegie Steel, U.S. Steel and Bethlehem Steel?

a) Henry Bessemer   c) Jay Gould
b) Andrew Carnegie   d) Charles Schwab

8. Who of the following helped the Cleveland administration solve a financial crisis brought about by the federal government's shrinking gold reserves?

a) William Jennings Bryan
b) James Fiske
c) J. P. Morgan
d) John D. Rockefeller

9. Who was the labor leader during the 1894 Pullman Rail strike, in which rioting led to eleven deaths following the arrival of government troops?

a) Bill Tilden   c) Joe Hill
b) Samuel Gompers   d) Eugene V. Debs

10. In what year did union membership as a percentage of the total U.S. labor force peak at 35.5%?

a) 1925   c) 1945
b) 1935   d) 1955

11. Under the leadership of William C. Durant, what was the largest U.S. automobile company in 1908?

a) Buick   c) Chevrolet
b) Cadillac   d) Oldsmobile

12. What was the name of the document that New York traders adopted in 1792, which was the effective beginning of the New York Stock Exchange?

a) The Walnut Tree Compact
b) The Buttonwood Agreement
c) The Lindenwood Charter
d) The Liberty Tree Contract

13. Where were both the first bank and the first stock exchange in the U.S. located?

a) Baltimore   c) New York
b) Boston   d) Philadelphia

14. What is the only stock that was part of the original Dow Jones list of the 1890s and is still a component of the list used to compute today's industrial average?

a) DuPont   c) Standard Oil
b) General Electric   d) U.S. Steel

15. In what year did the Dow Jones Average close above 1,000 for the first time?

a) 1960   c) 1968
b) 1964   d) 1972

16. At the peak of the Reagan-era bull market the Dow reached 2,722. It plunged 508 points in October of 1987. When did it first close above 3,000?

a) 1989   c) 1993
b) 1991   d) 1995

17. All of the companies used to compute the Dow Jones Average are traded on the New York Stock exchange except two. Name these two NASDAQ stocks.

18. Which of these stocks is not currently a component of the Dow Jones Average?

a) Coca-Cola   c) Pfizer
b) Walt Disney   d) Philip Morris

19. In which city did Frank Woolworth open his first successful 5- and 10-cent store in 1879?

a) Harrisburg, PA   c) Rochester, NY
b) Lancaster, PA   d) Watertown, NY

20. Match the historical business figure to the company with which he was associated:

A. Asa Chandler   1. N.Y. Central Railroad
B. James Duke   2. Alcoa
C. Amadeo Giannini   3. IBM
D. Edward Harriman   4. TWA
E. Howard Hughes   5. Standard Oil
F. Walter Jacobs   6. Bank of America
G. Ray Kroc   7. Coca-Cola
H. Andrew Mellon   8. American Tobacco
I. John D. Rockefeller   9. General Motors
J. Alfred P. Sloan   10. Hertz
K. Cornelius Vanderbilt 11. McDonalds
L. Thomas Watson   12. Union Pacific Railroad

Children's Literature

1. Which was published first, *The Adventures of Tom Sawyer* or *The Adventures of Huckleberry Finn?*

2. Which of these is not included in the title of a Harry Potter book?
   a) Chamber of Secrets
   b) Goblet of Fire
   c) Hidden Staircase
   d) Prisoner of Azkaban

3. Match the author to the book:

A. Margaret Wise Brown	1. *Hans Brinker and the Silver Skates*
B. Frances Hodgson Burnett	2. *Make Way for Ducklings*
C. Mary Mapes Dodge	3. *The Secret Garden*
D. Crockett Johnson	4. *Black Beauty*
E. Robert McClosky	5. *Mike Mulligan and His Steam Shovel*
F. L. M. Montgomery	6. *Goodnight Moon*
G. Anna Sewell	7. *Harold and the Purple Crayon*
H. Virginia Lee Burton	8. *Anne of Green Gables*

$4.$ Name the author of *Are You There God? It's Me Margaret,* *Superfudge* and *Tales of a Fourth Grade Nothing.*

$5.$ Identify the nationality of each of these authors:

    A. Louisa May Alcott
    B. Margaret Wise Brown
    C. Frances Hodgson Burnett
    D. Madeline L'Engle
    E. E. B. White

$6.$ What do the initials A. A. stand for in A. A. Milne?

    a) Arthur Anderson
    b) Andrew Astor
    c) Arnold Alsop
    d) Alan Alexander

$7.$ What are the names of the three volumes in the *Lord of the Rings* trilogy?

$8.$ Who is the author of *Henry Higgins* and the Ramona books?

$9.$ Put these authors in chronological order based upon their dates of birth:

    A. L. Frank Baum
    B. A. A. Milne
    C. Hans Christian Andersen
    D. Roald Dahl
    E. Dr. Seuss
    F. Jakob Grimm

10. Which of these is not a Beatrix Potter character?

a) Mopsy Cottontail
b) Wobbly Hedgehog
c) Squirrel Nutkin
d) Jemima Puddle-Duck

11. How many books are there in *The Chronicles of Narnia?*

a) 3   c) 7
b) 5   d) 9

12. What was the name of Sherlock Holmes's older brother?

13. Which of these is not a novel by H. G. Wells?

a) *The Time Machine*
b) *The Invisible Man*
c) *The War of the Worlds*
d) 20,000 *Leagues Under the Sea*

14. The Newberry Medal is awarded by the American Library Association for distinguished American literature for children. Match these award-winning books with their authors:

A. *Voyages of Dr. Doolittle*   1. Scott O'Dell
B. *Johnny Tremain*   2. William H. Armstrong
C. *Sounder*   3. Esther Forbes
D. *Island of the Blue Dolphins* 4. Hugh Lofting
E. *Sarah, Plain and Tall*   5. Katherine Paterson
F. *Julie of the Wolves*   6. Patricia MacLachlan
G. *Jacob Have I Loved*   7. Jean George

15. Which illustrator won the Caldecott award for the distinguished American picture book twice, first for *Jumanji* in 1982, and then for *Polar Express* in 1986?

16. What South African-born author taught Anglo-Saxon and Old English languages at Oxford University while creating the character of "Gollum," among many others?

17. Which of these is not a character in Archie comics?

a) Betty   c) Reggie
b) Clyde   d) Veronica

18. To what historic event does the nursery rhyme "Ring Around the Rosie" refer?

a) The Children's Crusade
b) The Easter Parade
c) The Fire of London
d) The Bubonic Plague

19. In the Harry Potter novels, what is the name for ordinary humans who possess no magical powers?

20. Which of these is not a book by Dr. Seuss?

a) *Are You My Mother?*
b) *The Cat in the Hat*
c) *Horton Hears a Who*
d) *Yertle the Turtle*

The Civil War

1. The Mason-Dixon line established the boundary between which two states?

   a) Maryland and Pennsylvania
   b) Virginia and Maryland
   c) Kentucky and Tennessee
   d) Missouri and Iowa

2. Who was a great-grandparent of Robert E. Lee's wife, Mary?

   a) Benjamin Franklin
   b) Thomas Jefferson
   c) Dolley Madison
   d) Martha Washington

3. Approximately how many battles were fought during the Civil War?

   a) 120   c) 1,200
   b) 220   d) 2,200

4. In which state was the greatest number of battles fought?

   a) Georgia   c) Maryland
   b) Kentucky   d) Virginia

5. Of the eleven state legislatures voting to secede, which three conducted referendums confirming the decision by a majority of the state's popular vote?

6. What state legislature voted not to secede by a 53 to 13 majority in April, 1861?

    a) Kentucky   c) Maryland
    b) Missouri   d) California

7. What new state entered the Union on June 20, 1863?

8. Who was the vice president of the Confederacy?

9. Who was the secretary of state for the Confederacy?

    a) Rufus Anderson
    b) Judah Benjamin
    c) Hamilton J. Culpepper
    d) Joseph Lumpkin

10. Approximately how many total deaths did Union forces incur both as a result of battles and other causes?

    a) 165,000   c) 565,000
    b) 365,000   d) 765,000

11. Approximately how many Confederates died in battle?

    a) 75,000   c) 275,000
    b) 175,000   d) 375,000

12. Lincoln's running mate in 1864, Andrew Johnson, had not supported Lincoln in the prior election. Which candidate had Johnson supported in 1860?

a) John Bell   c) Stephen Douglas

b) John Breckinridge   d) Millard Fillmore

13. Which one-time U.S. president was public in his sympathy for the Confederacy, in which four of his sons served?

a) Millard Fillmore   c) John Tyler

b) Franklin Pierce   d) Martin Van Buren

14. Who do the following points describe? (And how many does it take for you to identify him?)

A. Born in Mississippi

B. West Point graduate

C. U.S. Senator

D. Secretary of War

E. Elected in Montgomery

F. Served in Richmond

G. Captured in Georgia

15. What was the ironclad ship Merrimack renamed when it was salvaged by the Confederate Navy?

a) *The Robert E. Lee*

b) *The Southern Star*

c) *The Virginia*

d) *The George Washington*

16.
What was the first Confederate state capital to fall to Union forces, in February 1862?

a) Jackson   c) New Orleans
b) Nashville   d) Raleigh

17.
What was the name of Robert E. Lee's horse?

a) Tallyrand   c) Trigger
b) Traveler   d) Tupelo

18.
In February 1865, the last remaining Confederate port fell to Union forces. Where was it?

a) Charleston, SC
b) Galveston, TX
c) Jacksonville, FL
d) Wilmington, NC

19.
What was the name of the Confederate submarine that sank in Charleston Harbor after taking down the Union vessel Housatonic?

a) Babcock   c) H. L. Hunley
b) Calhoun   d) Walton

20.
Who was the featured speaker at Gettysburg just before Abraham Lincoln gave his brief, but famous, address?

a) James Blaine   c) Edward Everett
b) Salmon Chase   d) Thaddeus Stevens

Classical Music and Opera

1. Which of these instruments would you not expect to be included in a symphony orchestra?

   a) Bassoon   c) Tuba
   b) Saxophone   d) Xylophone

2. Founded in 1842, what is the oldest major orchestra in the United States?

   a) Boston Symphony Orchestra
   b) National Symphony, Washington, DC
   c) New York Philharmonic
   d) Philadelphia Orchestra

3. Put these composers in chronological order by birth date:

   A. Johann Sebastian Bach
   B. Ludwig van Beethoven
   C. Johannes Brahms
   D. Richard Strauss

4. Which musical tempo means "fast"?

   a) Adagio   c) Largo
   b) Allegro   d) Presto

5. Name the five stringed instruments you would expect to be included in a symphony orchestra.

6. How many strings does a violin have?

   a) 4   c) 6
   b) 5   d) 7

7. Match the opera to its composer:

   A. *Rigoletto*   1. Henry Purcell
   B. *La Boheme*   2. Englebert Humperdinck
   C. *The Fairy Queen*   3. Wolfgang Amadeus Mozart
   D. *Carmen*   4. Richard Strauss
   E. *Barber of Seville*   5. Georges Bizet
   F. *Die Fledermaus*   6. Giuseppe Verdi
   G. *Don Giovanni*   7. Richard Wagner
   H. *Parsifal*   8. Giacomo Puccini
   I. *Elektra*   9. Johann Strauss
   J. *Hansel & Gretel*   10. Gioacchino Rossini

8. What composer won a Pulitzer prize in 1945 for his *Appalachian Spring*?

9. What instrument links Pablo Casals, Jacqueline DuPre and Yo-Yo Ma?

10. The English horn is a low-pitched variation of which other instrument?

    a) French horn   c) Piccolo
    b) Oboe   d) Tuba

11. What instrument, named for its inventor, combines an oboe's keys with a clarinet's mouthpiece?

12. Match the composer with his nationality:

    A. Leonard Bernstein   1. French
    B. Frederick Chopin   2. American
    C. Edvard Grieg   3. German
    D. George Handel   4. Hungarian
    E. Franz Liszt   5. Austrian
    F. Maurice Ravel   6. English
    G. Arthur Sullivan   7. Polish
    H. Franz Haydn   8. Norwegian

13. What soprano, born in Laurel, MS in 1927, achieved fame performing in *Porgy and Bess, Aida* and *Madame Butterfly*?

    a) Jessye Norman
    b) Marian Anderson
    c) Roberta Peters
    d) Leontyne Price

14. Who was born in Venice in 1678 and is remembered for his concertos including *La Quattro Stagioni?*

15. Which composer wrote the opera *Nixon in China?*

    a) John Adams   c) John Cage
    b) Samuel Barber   d) Virgil Thomson

16. What American composer wrote the operas *Einstein on the Beach* and *The Voyage*?

17. Which of these operas was composed by Vincenzo Bellini?

a) *Aida*   c) *La Sonnambula*

b) *La Traviata*   d) *Tosca*

18. Ludwig van Beethoven was a student of which composer?

a) George Handel   c) Franz Schubert

b) Joseph Haydn   d) Antonio Vivaldi

19. What is the popular name for Beethoven's Piano Sonata, Opus 13?

a) "Emperor"   c) "Moonlight"

b) "Eroica"   d) "Pathetique"

20. Match the work to its composer:

A. *Jeremiah Symphony*   1. Edvard Grieg

B. *Fanfare for the Common Man* 2. Gustav Holst

C. *Sorcerer's Apprentice*   3. Igor Stravinsky

D. *New World Symphony*   4. Richard Strauss

E. *Peer Gynt Suite*   5. Aaron Copland

F. *The Planets*   6. Paul Dukas

G. *Peter and the Wolf*   7. Leonard Bernstein

H. *William Tell*   8. Nikolai Rimsky-Korsakov

I. *Thus Spake Zarathustra*   9. Sergei Prokofiev

J. *The Rite of Spring*   10. Antonin Dvorak

K. *The Sleeping Beauty*   11. Gioacchino Rossini

L. *Flight of the Bumblebee*   12. Peter Tchaikovsky

Computers

1. What was the full name for the UNIVAC machine created in 1951?

2. Who was the first major customer for the UNIVAC, which used magnetic tape rather than punch cards?
   a) Department of Defense
   b) NASA
   c) Prudential Life Insurance
   d) The Census Bureau

3. Which company successfully competed with UNIVAC beginning in 1955 with its 700 Series computer?
   a) Remington Rand
   b) IBM
   c) Honeywell
   d) Hewlett-Packard

4. What was the name of the four-computer network developed by the Department of Defense that became the earliest form of the Internet?
   a) DEFNET   c) ARNAVNET
   b) ARPANET   d) AFNET

5. What Internet domain name is preferred for nonprofit entities?

6. What does the acronym "COBOL" mean?

7. What does the acronym "BASIC" mean?

8. In what year did the U.S. Census first use punch-card technology?

   a) 1890   c) 1930
   b) 1910   d) 1950

9. In what year did Microsoft first release its Windows operating system?

   a) 1980   c) 1990
   b) 1985   d) 1995

10. Which of these companies is not based in the Silicon Valley area of California?

   a) Apple   c) Hewlett-Packard
   b) Dell   d) Intel

11. Match the business leader with his company:

   A. Jeff Bezos   1. AOL
   B. Steve Case   2. Apple
   C. John Chambers   3. Intel
   D. Andrew Grove   4. IBM
   E. Thomas Watson   5. Cisco Systems
   F. Steve Wozniak   6. Amazon

12. What does the acronym "HTML" mean?

13. What does the acronym "RAM" mean?

14. In what year did IBM enter the personal computer market?

a) 1981   c) 1985
b) 1983   d) 1987

15. What technological device was invented by William Schockley?

a) microchip
b) transistor
c) vacuum tube
d) AC/DC regulator

16. What was the name of the IBM computer that defeated chess champion Gary Kasparov in 1997?

a) Blue King   c) Blue Knight
b) Big Blue   d) Deep Blue

17. Rank these computer makers from largest to smallest based upon annual revenue in the year 2000:

A. Apple
B. Dell
C. Gateway
D. IBM

18. Who invented the first "automatic computer" in 1830?

a) Herman Hollerith
b) Blaise Pascal
c) William Compton
d) Charles Babbage

19. Who was the founder of both Netscape and Silicon Graphics?

20. What is the name of the free PC operating system developed in Sweden?

Film and Hollywood

1. Name the three films that each won all five of the following major Academy Awards: Best Picture, Best Actor, Best Actress, Best Director, Best Screenplay. The winning films were in 1934, 1975 and 1991.

2. Who is the only winner of the Best Actor award to have also directed himself in the winning role?

   a) Warren Beatty   c) Laurence Olivier
   b) Kevin Costner   d) Orson Wells

3. Match the Marx Brother with his legal name:

   A. Chico   1. Julius
   B. Groucho   2. Adolph
   C. Gummo   3. Herbert
   D. Harpo   4. Leonard
   E. Zeppo   5. Milton

4. Which of these screen stars did not have an affair with Howard Hughes?

a) Katherine Hepburn   c) Judy Garland
b) Ava Gardner   d) Rita Hayworth

5. Samuel Goldwyn, famous for his malapropisms, adopted the name "Goldwyn." What was his last name before it was Goldwyn?

a) Goldfinch   c) Goldfish
b) Goldberg   d) Goldstein

6. How many frames per second are there in 35mm movie film?

a) 8 frames/second
b) 16 frames/second
c) 24 frames/second
d) 36 frames/second

7. Who of the following was not one of the founders of United Artists in 1919?

a) Charlie Chaplin   c) Mary Pickford
b) D. W. Griffith   d) Rudolph Valentino

8. What does the "gaffer" do on a film set?

9. Match the mogul to his studio:

A. Harry Cohn   1. MGM
B. Howard Hughes   2. Columbia
C. Carl Laemmle   3. 20th Century Fox
D. Louis Mayer   4. Universal
E. Daryl Zanuck   5. Paramount
F. Adolph Zukor   6. RKO

10. Which of these movies was not one in which Katherine Hepburn won a Best Actress award?

    a) *Morning Glory*
    b) *The Philadelphia Story*
    c) *Guess Who's Coming to Dinner*
    d) *On Golden Pond*

11. What was the name of Marilyn Monroe's character in *Some Like it Hot?* (Hint: The one that always got "the fuzzy end of the lollipop.")

12. Who did the singing for Deborah Kerr in *The King and I,* for Natalie Wood in *West Side Story,* and for Audrey Hepburn in *My Fair Lady?*

13. What was the first Fred Astaire-Ginger Rogers movie in 1933?

    a) *Flying Down to Rio*   c) *Swing Time*
    b) *Shall We Dance*   d) *Top Hat*

14. Who was nominated for twelve best directing awards, more than any other director?

    a) John Ford   c) William Wyler
    b) Billy Wilder   d) Fred Zinnemann

15. What prolific costume designer won eight Academy Awards from her thirty-five nominations?

16. In 1944 and 1945, long before Coppola's *The Godfather,* Leo McCarey directed a film and its sequel that were both nominated for Best Picture. Name the two films and identify the film that won the Best Picture award.

17. Match the director to the film for which he won an Academy Award:

A. Elia Kazan	1.	*Mrs. Miniver*
B. Delbert Mann	2.	*A Letter to Three Wives*
C. Joseph Mankiewicz	3.	*Gentleman's Agreement*
D. Tony Richardson	4.	*From Here to Eternity*
E. Franklin Schaffner	5.	*A Place in the Sun*
F. George Stevens	6.	*Marty*
G. William Wyler	7.	*Patton*
H. Fred Zinnemann	8.	*Tom Jones*

18. Match the Best Picture winner with its studio:

A. *Amadeus*	1.	RKO
B. *Annie Hall*	2.	MGM
C. *Ben Hur*	3.	Universal
D. *The Best Years of Our Lives*	4.	Miramax
E. *Casablanca*	5.	Fox
F. *The English Patient*	6.	Paramount
G. *The Godfather*	7.	Warner Brothers
H. *It Happened One Night*	8.	United Artists
I. *Patton*	9.	Orion
J. *Schindler's List*	10.	Columbia

19. Four musicals won the Best Picture award during the 1960s. Name the winners for each year:

A. 1961	C.	1965
B. 1964	D.	1968

20. Who was nominated as Best Director five times but never won the award—although one of his films won the Best Picture award in 1940?

First Ladies

1. Which of the first four first ladies was not a widow when she married a future president?

   a) Martha Washington

   b) Abigail Adams

   c) Martha Jefferson

   d) Dolley Madison

2. Four presidents were widowers when they entered the White House. Which of the following first ladies lived to see her husband become president?

   a) Martha Jefferson

   b) Hannah Van Buren

   c) Sarah Polk

   d) Ellen Arthur

3. Although she was raised in a strict Quaker home, which first lady became well known for her fashionable clothes, parties and her habit of taking snuff?

   a) Martha Washington

   b) Abigail Adams

   c) Elizabeth Monroe

   d) Dolley Madison

4. Which of these first ladies did not get married to her husband during his term as President?

   a) Edith Roosevelt

   b) Julia Tyler

   c) Edith Wilson

   d) Frances Cleveland

5. Who was the first presidential wife to live in the White House?

   a) Martha Washington   c) Martha Jefferson
   b) Abigail Adams   d) Dolley Madison

6. While her husband was the U.S. minister to France, which future first lady helped save Madame de Lafayette, who was a prisoner of the French Revolution?

   a) Martha Jefferson   c) Louisa Adams
   b) Abigail Adams   d) Elizabeth Monroe

7. Which first lady grew up in Europe, the daughter of an American father and a British mother who met her husband when he was U.S. minister to the Netherlands?

   a) Louisa Adams   c) Julia Tyler
   b) Hannah Van Buren   d) Sarah Polk

8. Who was the mother of ten children and lived to the age of 88 but was only first lady for 31 days?

9. Which of these women was not one of the five first ladies whose maiden name was "Smith"?

   a) Abigail Adams   c) Ida McKinley
   b) Rosalyn Carter   d) Margaret Taylor

10. Who was the only first lady who married one president and was the grandmother of another?

   a) Abigail Adams   c) Anna Harrison
   b) Edith Roosevelt   d) Barbara Bush

11.
Which future first lady and her husband met as students (she was twenty-one years old, he nineteen) at the same school in the winter of 1818?

a) Anna Harrison   c) Margaret Taylor
b) Sarah Polk   d) Abigail Fillmore

12.
Which first lady was given the nickname "Lemonade" because she did not permit alcoholic beverages to be served in the White House?

13.
Match the first lady with her presidential husband:

A. Julia Dent	1. Lyndon Johnson
B. Helen Herron	2. Herbert Hoover
C. Lucretia Rudolph	3. Warren Harding
D. Lou Henry	4. Ulysses Grant
E. Jane Appleton	5. Calvin Coolidge
F. Florence Kling DeWolfe	6. Richard Nixon
G. Grace Goodhue	7. Gerald Ford
H. Claudia Taylor	8. William Taft
I. Thelma Ryan	9. James Garfield
J. Elizabeth Warren	10. Franklin Pierce

14.
Who was the youngest first lady? She was only twenty-one when she married the forty-eight-year-old president.

a) Frances Cleveland   c) Edith Roosevelt
b) Julia Tyler   d) Ida McKinley

15.
Which first lady suffered from epilepsy and was a near invalid during her time in the White House?

a) Ida McKinley   c) Lucy Hayes
b) Edith Roosevelt   d) Abigail Fillmore

16. The Baby Ruth candy bar is rumored to be named for the daughter of which first lady?

   a) Frances Cleveland   c) Eleanor Roosevelt
   b) Edith Roosevelt   d) Edith Wilson

17. Which first lady had five children in addition to the young stepdaughter from her husband's first marriage?

   a) Edith Roosevelt   c) Alice Roosevelt
   b) Eleanor Roosevelt   d) Nancy Reagan

18. Who was the first future first lady to earn a college degree when she graduated from the Wesleyan Female College of Cincinnati?

   a) Edith Roosevelt   c) Eleanor Roosevelt
   b) Mary Todd Lincoln   d) Lucy Hayes

19. Which future first lady worked at the Washington Times-Herald as their "Inquiring Camera Girl"?

   a) Eleanor Roosevelt   c) Elizabeth Wallace
   b) Jacqueline Bouvier   d) Mamie Doud

20. Who was the first first lady to have been born in the twentieth century?

   a) Jacqueline Kennedy   c) Pat Nixon
   b) Ladybird Johnson   d) Bess Truman

Food

1. Which beverage was originally sold as "Brad's Drink" in North Carolina during the 1890s?

   a) Coca-Cola
   b) Dr. Pepper
   c) Pepsi-Cola
   d) Royal Crown cola

2. The greatest amount of saturated fat will be found in a tablespoon of which of these foods?

   a) Mayonnaise
   b) Olive oil
   c) Peanut butter
   d) Sour cream

3. What is the process involved in creating "extra virgin" olive oil?

4. Which of these items is not included on a McDonald's Big Mac?

   a) Ketchup
   b) Lettuce
   c) Onions
   d) Pickles

5. In which cooking technique does one plunge food into boiling water for a very brief time?

a) Basting
b) Blanching
c) Poaching
d) Scalding

6. What powdery baking ingredient is derived from the acid residue of the wine making process?

7. Which of these fish has a high fat content compared to the others?

a) Amberjack
b) Cod
c) Halibut
d) Red snapper

8. Which of these is not a variety of hard cheese?

a) Cheddar
b) Gorgonzola
c) Gouda
d) Swiss

9. How many cups are contained in a gallon?

10. "Parsley, sage, rosemary and thyme" are

a) Herbs
b) Spices
c) Half are spices and half are herbs
d) Neither spices, nor herbs

11. What food includes the following varieties: "banana,"
"hubbard," "spaghetti" and "sweet dumpling"?

12. Who first described coffee from Nashville's Maxwell House
as being "good to the last drop"?

a) P. T. Barnum
b) Sarah Bernhardt
c) William Jennings Bryan
d) Theodore Roosevelt

13. Which treat was introduced to the American public at the
1904 World's Fair in St. Louis?

a) Cotton candy
b) French fries
c) Ice-cream cones
d) Pizza

14. What dish consists of diced apples, celery, nuts and
mayonnaise?

15. Which of these fast food chains is not part of the Tricon
Global restaurant group?

a) Arby's
b) Kentucky Fried Chicken
c) Pizza Hut
d) Taco Bell

16. What is the primary ingredient in hummus?

17. Which of these is not one of the spices typically used in curry powder?

   a) Cumin
   b) Marjoram
   c) Pepper
   d) Turmeric

18. Which of these dishes is a highly seasoned thick stew with meat, poultry or fish?

   a) Bisque
   b) Bouillabaisse
   c) Fricassee
   d) Ragout

19. The salad named after Cesar Cardini was created in his restaurant in which country?

   a) Mexico
   b) Monaco
   c) Morocco
   d) United States

20. Which of these food brands is not owned by the Philip Morris Company?

   a) Jell-O
   b) Jif
   c) Oreo
   d) Oscar Mayer

Games
and Toys

1. What casino game is also known as "Chemin de Fer"?

   a) Blackjack   c) Baccarat
   b) Roulette   d) Craps

2. What lawn game uses a shuttlecock?

3. How many points do you earn for your first Yahtzee?

   a) 25   c) 50
   b) 40   d) 100

4. What are the names of the four railroad properties in Monopoly?

5. Which of the following Monopoly properties is not orange?

   a) Tennessee Avenue
   b) St. James Place
   c) New York Avenue
   d) St. Charles Place

6. In what card game is it desirable to "meld" the queen of
   spades with the jack of diamonds?

   a) Pinochle
   b) Bridge
   c) Hearts
   d) Spades

7. Which of these is not a Mattel-owned brand?

   a) Barbie
   b) Playskool
   c) Fisher-Price
   d) Hot Wheels

8. What number is added to roulette wheels in the U.S., but is
   not included in the European version of the game?

   a) 13
   b) 0
   c) 00
   d) 37

9. In a game of straight poker, what hands beat a flush?

10. In the first roll of a game of craps, what two numbers will
    be winners for pass-line bettors?

    a) 2 or 12
    b) 5 or 9
    c) 6 or 8
    d) 7 or 11

11. Which of these is not a racetrack betting option?

    a) Trifecta
    b) Perfecta
    c) Quinella
    d) Tripella

12. What implement is needed to play a game of "mumblety-peg"?

13. Whose son invented Lincoln Logs in 1916?

    a) Robert Todd Lincoln
    b) Theodore Roosevelt
    c) William Randolph Hearst
    d) Frank Lloyd Wright

14. Name the six suspects used to play a game of Clue.

15. In casino blackjack, what does the dealer do when his cards total 16?

16. In the game "Battleship," how many hits does it take to sink a submarine?

    a) 2   c) 4
    b) 3   d) 5

17. How many threes are included in a 48-card pinochle deck?

18. Which of these is not a term used in a game of bridge?

    a) Flunk
    b) Grand slam
    c) Knock-out
    d) Ruff

19. In which country were LEGO blocks created?

    a) Denmark
    b) Germany
    c) Sweden
    d) Switzerland

20. What are the names of each of the pieces in a chess game?

Geography

1. Put these U.S. cities in order from east to west:

   A. Charleston, SC
   B. Charleston, WV
   C. Charlotte, NC
   D. Chattanooga, TN
   E. Cleveland, OH
   F. Columbia, SC
   G. Columbus, GA
   H. Columbus, OH

2. Put these U.S. cities in order from north to south:

   A. Atlanta, GA
   B. Jackson, MS
   C. Los Angeles, CA
   D. Mobile, AL
   E. Nashville, TN
   F. Orlando, FL
   G. Raleigh, NC
   H. San Antonio, TX

3. Where is the northernmost point in North America?

   a) Alaska
   b) Greenland
   c) Northwest Territory, Canada
   d) Yukon Territory, Canada

4. Having left Washington, DC, and traveled due east across the Atlantic Ocean, near which of these European cities will you eventually arrive?

   a) Bordeaux, France
   b) Casablanca, Morocco
   c) Dakar, Senegal
   d) Lisbon, Portugal

5. Which two U.S. states share a border with eight other states?

6. What are the four states that meet to form a common point at the "Four Corners"?

7. Five states are bisected by the line between the eastern and central time zones. Which of these states is not in both time zones?

   a) Florida   c) Indiana
   b) Illinois   d) Michigan

8. True or false? Bristol, TN is closer to Canada than it is to Memphis, TN?

9. Which state shares a border with only one other state?

10. In which state are three of the four largest U.S. islands?

a) Alaska   c) Hawaii

b) Florida   d) Massachusetts

11. Which island was originally known as "Van Dieman's Land"?

a) Burma   c) New Guinea

b) Java   d) Tasmania

12. Place these northern hemisphere cities in order from north to south:

A. Athens, Greece

B. Berlin, Germany

C. London, England

D. Mexico City, Mexico

E. New Delhi, India

F. Tokyo, Japan

G. Toronto, Canada

H. Washington, DC

13. Which of these countries has fourteen international borders?

a) Afghanistan   c) Brazil

b) Austria   d) China

14. How many U.S. states share a border with Canada?

15. Based upon its physical size, what is the world's smallest nation?

16. Which of these islands is the largest?

a) Cuba   c) Iceland

b) Honshu   d) Ireland

17. Match the city with its body of water:

A. Cologne, Germany	1. Indian Ocean
B. Hamburg, Germany	2. Straits of Jurong
C. Istanbul, Turkey	3. Baltic Sea
D. Lisbon, Portugal	4. Port Philip Bay
E. Melbourne, Australia	5. Rhine River
F. Mogadishu, Somalia	6. Sea of Marma
G. Palermo, Sicily	7. Tyrrhenian Sea
H. St. Petersburg, Russia	8. Tagus River
I. Singapore (nation)	9. Gulf of Finland
J. Stockholm, Sweden	10. Elbe River

18. Having left Cairo, Egypt, and traveled due east through North Africa and across the Atlantic Ocean, near what U.S. city are you when you arrive on the shores of North America?

a) Charleston, SC
b) Jacksonville, FL
c) Savannah, GA
d) Wilmington, NC

19. Which of these islands does Indonesia share with Malaysia?

a) Bali   c) Java
b) Borneo   d) Sumatra

20. Which of these is not an Irish county?

a) Blarney   c) Limerick
b) Galway   d) Sligo

Government

1. Which of these countries is not a member of the United Nations?

   a) Slovenia   c) Sweden
   b) Somalia   d) Switzerland

2. How many U.N. members were there in 2002?

   a) 185   c) 192
   b) 189   c) 198

3. In what city was the U.N. charter developed and signed?

   a) Geneva   c) Paris
   b) New York   d) San Francisco

4. Which of the following men was not a U.S. Representative to the United Nations?

   a) Henry Cabot Lodge Jr.
   b) Adlai Stevenson
   c) Dean Rusk
   d) George H. W. Bush

$5.$ The U.N. Security Council consists of fifteen countries, including which five permanent members?

$6.$ The European Economic Community began in 1958 with six countries. Name them.

$7.$ Which of these nations is not currently a member of the European Union?

a) Finland   c) Norway
b) Greece   d) Portugal

$8.$ Which is the only country in Southeast Asia to have avoided European colonization during the fifteenth through twentieth centuries?

a) Burma   c) Malaysia
b) Cambodia   d) Thailand

$9.$ Name the group of Spanish-governed islands in the Mediterranean that includes Ibiza?

$10.$ "The Commonwealth" is a free association of independent nations formerly subject to British rule. How many nations belong to the Commonwealth?

a) 24   c) 44
b) 34   d) 54

$11.$ Which president used his veto power over Congress more than any other?

a) Andrew Jackson
b) Franklin Roosevelt
c) Ronald Reagan
d) Harry Truman

12. Who was Richard Nixon's first secretary of state?

a) Alexander Haig
b) Henry Kissinger
c) Elliot Richardson
d) William Rogers

13. Which of the following women was not a member of George W. Bush's original cabinet in 2001?

a) Elaine Chao
b) Gale Norton
c) Ann Veneman
d) Christine Todd Whitman

14. Which of these is an independent nation, rather than a British Overseas Territory?

a) Anguilla
b) Barbados
c) Bermuda
d) Cayman Islands

15. Which of these nations is not governed as a constitutional monarchy?

a) Belgium
b) Denmark
c) Luxembourg
d) Portugal

16. Put these ruling dynasties of China in chronological order:

A. Chin
B. Ming
C. Qing
D. Yuan

17. What is the minimum age requirement to become a member of the U.S. Senate?

a) 25   c) 35
b) 30   d) 40

18. Who was the only speaker of the House of Representatives (he served during the 24th and 25th Congresses) to later become president of the United States?

19. Which of these families was not one of the ruling dynasties of the Holy Roman Empire?

a) Bourbon
b) Carolingian
c) Habsburg
d) Hohenstaufen

20. Rebecca Felton, the first woman appointed to serve in the U.S. Senate, represented which state?

a) Arkansas
b) Georgia
c) Mississippi
d) Montana

Higher Education

1. When was the U.S. Military Academy at West Point founded?

   a) 1782   c) 1802

   b) 1792   d) 1812

2. Where is the U.S. Coast Guard Academy located?

   a) Annapolis, MD
   b) Kings Point, NY
   c) New London, CT
   d) Newport, RI

3. Which Puritan minister was one of the founders of Yale University?

   a) John Coffin
   b) Jonathan Edwards
   c) Cotton Mather
   d) Roger Williams

4. Which U.S. college was one of the first to adopt coeducation?

   a) Bowdoin   c) Northeastern
   b) Lesley   d) Oberlin

5. At which midwestern state university did Dr. Alfred Kinsey develop his study of American sexual habits?

   a) Illinois   c) Iowa
   b) Indiana   d) Michigan

6. Which university established the first professional school of journalism?

   a) Columbia c) Missouri
   b) Michigan d) Northwestern

7. What university administers the Peabody Awards?

8. Approximately how many total public schools (elementary and secondary) are there in the United States?

   a) 46,000   c) 126,000
   b) 86,000   d) 166,000

9. Which of these European universities is the oldest?

   a) Bologna   c) Cologne
   b) Cambridge d) Oxford

10. Which of these countries has the greatest number of university students?

   a) China   c) Russia
   b) India   d) United States

11. What was Columbia University's original name?

12. Which of these universities is not a member of the Southeastern Conference?

    a) Florida   c) Georgia
    b) Florida State d) South Carolina

13. Which of these is not an Ivy League school?

    a) Brown   c) Duke
    b) Columbia   d) University of Pennsylvania

14. What university administers the Pulitzer Prizes?

15. Princeton and Columbia both had university presidents who went on to become U.S. presidents. Who were they?

16. Which was the first state-chartered university in the U.S.?

    a) Georgia   c) South Carolina
    b) Maryland   d) Virginia

17. What does the university degree D.D. designate?

18. Which of these universities is not among the top ten in terms of the number of students?

    a) Florida   c) Ohio State
    b) Michigan   d) Texas

19. Which U.S. president received his law degree from Duke University?

    a) Jimmy Carter   c) Gerald Ford
    b) Bill Clinton   d) Richard Nixon

20. Match the college to the location of its main campus:

A.	Bowdoin	1.	Philadelphia, PA
B.	Brandeis	2.	Waterville, ME
C.	Bucknell	3.	Lewisburg, PA
D.	Colby	4.	Omaha, NE
E.	Creighton	5.	St. Petersburg, FL
F.	Drake	6.	St. Augustine, FL
G.	Eckerd	7.	Deland, FL
H.	Flagler	8.	Waltham, MA
I.	Holy Cross	9.	Birmingham, AL
J.	Holy Family	10.	Brunswick, ME
K.	Samford	11.	Des Moines, IA
L.	Stetson	12.	Worcester, MA

Human Body

1. How many bones are there in a typical human adult?

2. Approximately how many bones does a newborn human have before the bones begin to fuse together?

   a) 250   c) 350
   b) 300   d) 400

3. What is the name of the smallest human bone, which is found in the ear?

   a) hammer   c) saddle
   b) drum   d) stirrup

4. In what part of the body are the parietal and temporal bones located?

5. Which vertebrae group contains the most bones?

   a) Cervical   c) Lumbar
   b) Thoracic   d) Pelvic

6. Match the bone with its location in the body:

A.	Femur	1.	Upper arm
B.	Fibula	2.	Skull
C.	Humerus	3.	Jaw
D.	Maxilla	4.	Shoulder
E.	Scapula	5.	Upper leg
F.	Sternum	6.	Chest
G.	Ulna	7.	Lower leg
H.	Zygomatic	8.	Lower arm

7. Which is the "master gland" of the endocrine system?

a) Thyroid   c) Thymus
b) Pituitary   d) Pancreas

8. Into which organ does the renal artery flow?

9. Which of these is not a part of the human hand?

a) Patellas   c) Metacarpals
b) Phalanges   d) Carpals

10. Which blood type is the universal donor that can be received by all other types?

11. Which blood type can receive all the other types?

12. What was the life expectancy of a child born in the United States in 2002?

a) 73   c) 83
b) 77   d) 87

1 3. What part of the body includes the pleura and the bronchus?

1 4. What is the name of the cell division that is unique to sperm and egg cells?

1 5. Adductors, intercostal and soleus are all examples of what tissues?

1 6. What body part includes dentin, pulp and cementum?

1 7. During the Middle Ages, what four body fluids were known as the "humors"?

1 8. Which side of the brain is associated with creativity and imagination?

1 9. What is the wrinkled outer layer of the brain?

2 0. Which type of brain wave is associated with deep sleep?

    a) Alpha   c) Theta
    b) Beta   d) Delta

Inventions

1. What two metals are combined to make bronze?

   a) Copper and tin   c) Zinc and tin

   b) Iron and zinc   d) Copper and zinc

2. In approximately what year did Gutenberg invent movable type?

   a) 1347   c) 1547

   b) 1447   d) 1647

3. Who is traditionally considered the inventor of the fountain pen in 1884?

   a) James Schaefer   c) George Cross

   b) William Parker   d) Lewis Waterman

4. What was the name of the first steamship to successfully cross the Atlantic Ocean?

   a) Savannah   c) Baltimore

   b) Charleston   d) Chesapeake

5. What automobile company invented the 3-point seat belt in 1959?

a) Ford   c) Saab
b) Fiat   d) Volvo

6. True or false? The Pilgrims on the Mayflower used a sextant to help guide them to North America.

7. In what year did Eli Whitney invent the cotton gin?

a) 1776   c) 1811
b) 1793   d) 1828

8. What did Alessandro Volta invent in 1800?

a) Circuit breaker
b) Electromagnet
c) Electric fuse
d) Electric battery

9. Who discovered X-rays, earning the first Nobel Prize for physics?

a) Marie Curie
b) Enrico Fermi
c) Wilhelm Conrad Roentgen
d) Nikola Tesla

10. Prior to inventing the magnetic telegraph in 1837, what had been Samuel Morse's profession?

a) Painter   c) Newspaper editor
b) Architect   d) Teacher

11. Which of the following items was not invented by Thomas Edison?

    a) Phonograph
    b) Kinetoscope
    c) Alternating current motor
    d) Electronic lamp

12. In which country are the Nobel prizes awarded?

13. The best-selling book *Longitude* followed the development of the chronometer by what inventor?

    a) George Harrison
    b) John Harrison
    c) George O'Hara
    d) James Harris

14. What was the name of the musical instrument invented by Benjamin Franklin?

15. Which was invented first, the Otis elevator, the Winchester rifle or the Bell telephone?

16. After the introduction of the assembly line to the Ford plant in 1913, how long did it take to build a Model T?

    a) 60 minutes   c) 3 hours
    b) 90 minutes   d) 6 hours

17. Who was nicknamed "The Wizard of Menlo Park"?

18. Celluloid was invented in 1870 by John Wesley Hyatt and Isaiah Hyatt because of a shortage of ivory for use in making what?

a) Piano keys   c) False teeth
b) Hair combs   d) Billiard balls

19. What did the Montgolfier brothers invent in 1783?

a) Golf balls
b) Hot air balloon
c) Spinning mule
d) Typewriter

20. Who invented the pneumatic tire in 1888?

a) Dunlop   c) Goodyear
b) Firestone   d) Michelin

Jazz

1. Which of these songs was not written by George and Ira Gershwin?

    a) "Embraceable You"
    b) "Oh, Lady Be Good"
    c) "I Got Rhythm"
    d) "I've Got My Love to Keep Me Warm"

2. Although she never recorded with them, with which band did Billie Holiday perform in 1937 and 1938?

    a) Count Basie   c) Fletcher Henderson
    b) Duke Ellington   d) Benny Goodman

3. What lyricist wrote "On the Sunny Side of the Street", "I'm in the Mood for Love" and "I Can't Give You Anything But Love, Baby"?

    a) Cole Porter   c) Harold Arlen
    b) Irving Berlin   d) Dorothy Fields

4. Which popular Billie Holiday song is about a lynching?

5. Who wrote the Artie Shaw hit "Begin the Beguine"?

   a) Cole Porter
   b) Irving Berlin
   c) George Gershwin
   d) Artie Shaw

6. What state were both Cole Porter and Hoagy Carmichael from?

   a) Georgia   c) Pennsylvania
   b) Virginia   d) Indiana

7. Before starting his own band, for whose band did Gene Krupa play drums?

   a) Glenn Miller
   b) Benny Goodman
   c) Artie Shaw
   d) Duke Ellington

8. Who wrote "Stardust"?

   a) Hoagy Carmichael
   b) Cole Porter
   c) George Gershwin
   d) Louis Armstrong

9. Which of these singers was born first?

   a) Ella Fitzgerald
   b) Billie Holiday
   c) Sarah Vaughan
   d) Dinah Washington

10. What New Orleans-born bandleader wrote "Sing, Sing, Sing"?

   a) Benny Goodman
   b) Louis Armstrong
   c) Louis Prima
   d) Gene Krupa

11. What trombone-playing bandleader had Frank Sinatra as a singer and Buddy Rich as a drummer?

12. Who was the French/Belgian musician widely regarded as one of the world's greatest guitar players?

13. Which singer's nickname was "The Velvet Fog"?

14. Which group made what is considered the first jazz record in 1917?

   a) Original Dixieland Jazz Band
   b) Louis Armstrong's Hot Five
   c) Jelly Roll Morton and his Red Hot Peppers
   d) The Creole Jazz Band

15. What bandleader was Louis Armstrong's early mentor?

   a) Wild Bill Davison
   b) W. C. Handy
   c) King Oliver
   d) Buddy Bolden

16. What instrument did Louis Armstrong's wife, Lil, play on many of the original Hot Five recordings?

   a) Trumpet   c) Banjo
   b) Saxophone   d) Piano

17. What was Duke Ellington's real name?

18. Which of these musicians was not a bass player?
  a) Chick Webb
  b) Walter Page
  c) Jimmy Blanton
  d) Harry Goodman

19. What instrument does Dave Brubeck play on his 1960 hit record "Take Five"?

20. Match the instrument to the musician:

A. Alto saxophone	1. Woody Herman
B. Bass	2. Miles Davis
C. Clarinet	3. John Coltrane
D. Cornet	4. Thelonius Monk
E. Drums	5. Charlie Parker
F. Piano	6. Charles Mingus
G. Tenor saxophone	7. Bix Beiderbecke
H. Trumpet	8. Max Roach

Language

1. Identify the five-letter palindromes defined below:

    A. A Honda automobile

    B. A cousin to the canoe

    C. A brothel keeper

    D. The former rulers of Iran

    E. Musical performances by one person

2. In which country is Tagalog one of the primary languages?

    a) India   c) Philippines

    b) Indonesia   d) Sri Lanka

3. Which of these is not among the top five most widely used of the world's primary languages?

    a) English   c) Hindi

    b) French   d) Spanish

$4.$ In which country is Kannada spoken?

    a) India   c) Myanmar
    b) Indonesia   d) Nigeria

$5.$ Which U.S. state is a one-syllable word?

$6.$ What is the nautical origin of the word "POSH"?

$7.$ What is the origin of the phrase "To mind your Ps and Qs"?

$8..$ What three letters are used most often in written English?

$9.$ What three words are used most frequently in spoken English?

$10.$ Match the Latin phrase with its definition:

    A. ad hoc   1. for the time being
    B. bona fide   2. at first view
    C. cum laude   3. retroactively
    D. de facto   4. lacking sound mind
    E. ex post facto   5. for the purpose at hand
    F. in situ   6. in good faith
    G. mea culpa   7. with praise
    H. non compus mentis 8. in reality
    I. prima facie   9. in the original place
    J. pro tempore   10. through my fault

$11.$ Complete this series: alpha, bravo, charlie, delta—for E, F, G and H.

$12.$ What are the two official languages in Belgium?

13. Which country contains the largest Portuguese-speaking population?

14. What are the four official languages in Switzerland?

15. Match the country with its official language:

A. Bangladesh   1. Farsi
B. Brunei   2. Arabic
C. Iran   3. Malay
D. Iraq   4. Urdu
E. Pakistan   5. Bengali

16. What is a heteronym?

17. Which Native American devised an 86-character written Cherokee language in 1821?

18. Which of the following is not among the Indo-European family of languages?

a) Celtic   c) Slavic
b) Iranian d) Tibetan

19. In approximately what year did Louis Braille develop his reading system for the blind?

a) 1533   c) 1733
b) 1633   d) 1833

20. What is defined as "an unsegmentable, gliding speech sound varying continuously in phonetic quality but considered to be a single sound or phoneme"?

Law

1. Which Supreme Court justice served as chief U.S. counsel at the Nuremberg Trials?

   a) James Byrnes
   b) Felix Frankfurter
   c) Robert Jackson
   d) Joseph Lamar

2. Which Nazi defendant committed suicide during the Nuremberg trials?

   a) Hermann Goering
   b) Joachim von Ribbentrop
   c) Albert Speer
   d) Julius Streicher

3. Which of the following Supreme Court justices was a liberal New Deal democrat, and had also been a member of the Ku Klux Klan?

   a) Hugo Black
   b) William O. Douglas
   c) Felix Frankfurter
   d) Harlan Stone

4. Which future Supreme Court chief justice ran as the Republican presidential candidate in 1916?

5. Which British monarch introduced the jury trial to replace trials by combat or by torture?
   a) William I   c) Richard I
   b) Henry II   d) Richard II

6. What lawyer defended the British soldiers who were charged with murder following the Boston Massacre?

7. Who was the defending attorney in the Dayton, Tennessee, "Monkey Trial" in 1925?

8. Which justice served on the Supreme Court longer than any other?
   a) Hugo Black
   b) William O. Douglas
   c) Oliver Wendell Holmes Jr.
   d) John Marshall

9. If a work is created after January 1, 1978, for how many years after the death of an author does the copyright stand?
   a) 30   c) 70
   b) 50   d) 95

10. Who was the judge in the 1995 O. J. Simpson murder trial?

11. Which state was the first to adopt a written constitution?
   a) Maryland   c) Pennsylvania
   b) Massachusetts   d) Virginia

1 2. Who wrote the majority opinion that legalized abortion in the 1973 decision of Roe v. Wade?

a) Harry Blackmun
b) William Brennan
c) Warren Burger
d) Earl Warren

1 3. How many constitutional amendments have been adopted?

a) 27   c) 29
b) 28   d) 30

1 4. Who was the first chief justice of the Supreme Court?

a) William Cushing
b) John Jay
c) Peyton Randolph
d) Edmund Randolph

1 5. Which U.S. state has a unicameral legislature?

a) Louisiana
b) Nebraska
c) New Hampshire
d) Wyoming

1 6. What is the legal term for "wrongful act which results in injury to another's person, property or reputation"?

1 7. What is the Second Amendment to the constitution?

1 8. Which landmark 1803 Supreme Court decision established the practice of judicial review for the purpose of determining the constitutionality of legislative acts?

19. Who was the U.S. solicitor general who successfully challenged the principle of "separate but equal" in the landmark case of Brown v. Board of Education of Topeka?

20. True or false? In the federal court system a judge can overrule a jury's verdict in a civil case.

Literature and Shakespeare

1–5. From which play does each of these Shakespearean lines originate?

1. "I come to wive it wealthily in Padua."

2. "Lord, what fools these mortals be."

3. "To sleep: perchance to dream: ay, there's the rub."

4. "This was the most unkindest cut of all."

5. "The first thing we do, let's kill all the lawyers."

6. Which character in *Merchant of Venice* gave the "quality of mercy" speech?
   a) Shylock
   b) Antonio
   c) Leonardo
   d) Portia

7. Which of Shakespeare's plays includes the characters Cordelia, Goneril and Regan?

8. What was the pen name of the American author whose short story collections include both *The Four Million* and *Cabbages and Kings?*

9. Match the author to his/her book:

A. Charlotte Brontë	1. *Middlemarch*
B. Emily Brontë	2. *The Vicar of Wakefield*
C. Daniel Defoe	3. *Vanity Fair*
D. Jonathan Swift	4. *The Forsythe Saga*
E. George Eliot	5. *The Rise of Silas Lapham*
F. Henry Fielding	6. *Wuthering Heights*
G. John Galsworthy	7. *Robinson Crusoe*
H. Oliver Goldsmith	8. *Tom Jones*
I. William Dean Howells	9. *Barchester Towers*
J. Lawrence Sterne	10. *Jane Eyre*
K. William Makepeace Thackery	11. *Gulliver's Travels*
L. Anthony Trollope	12. *Tristam Shandy*

10. What are the names of the lion statues on the steps of the main branch of the New York Public Library?

    a) Truth and Justice
    b) Liberty and Knowledge
    c) Patience and Fortitude
    d) Gertrude and Lawrence

11. In what novel does the character Gregor Samsa wake up as a cockroach?

12. Who won the Nobel Prize for literature in 1930, the first American to do so?

    a) Sinclair Lewis   c) Pearl S. Buck

    b) Eugene O' Neill   d) John Steinbeck

13. Which of these is not a book by F. Scott Fitzgerald?

    a) *The Beautiful and the Damned*

    b) *This Side of Paradise*

    c) *Tales of the Jazz Age*

    d) *The Lost Generation*

14. What is the name of the hero in *The Call of the Wild?*

15. Who is the most recent American author to have won both a Nobel Prize for literature and a Pulitzer Prize?

    a) John Updike   c) Saul Bellow

    b) Toni Morrison   d) Alice Walker

16. What was the name of the family of "Okies" who travel to California in John Steinbeck's *The Grapes of Wrath?*

17. Which novel was the first successful work by Charles Dickens when it was published in 1836?

    a) *A Christmas Carol*

    b) *David Copperfield*

    c) *The Pickwick Papers*

    d) *Oliver Twist*

18. Who was the industrialist who coauthored *The Communist Manifesto* with Karl Marx in 1848?

19. Who was the narrator of F. Scott Fitzgerald's *The Great Gatsby?*

a) Daisy Buchanan   c) Jay Gatsby

b) Nick Carraway   d) Eugene Grant

20. Which of these is not a collection of stories by Ring Lardner?

a) *Gullible's Travels*

b) *There's One Born Every Minute*

c) *Treat 'em Rough*

d) *You Know Me, Al*

Mathematics

1. What Greek mathematician proposed the theory that "in any right triangle, the square of the hypotenuse is equal to the sum of the squares on the other two sides"?

2. Who postulated that only one line may be drawn through a given point parallel to a given line?

3. Which Greek mathematician invented the "screw" method for raising water?

   a) Archimedes   c) Eudoxus
   b) Diophantus   d) Ptolemy

4. Which culture first developed the use of the zero in mathematics?

   a) Chinese   c) Hindu
   b) Egyptian   d) Phoenician

5. What is the sum of 166 and 122 when expressed as a roman numeral?

6. Who was the eleventh-century Persian poet of the *Rubaiyat* who also corrected the calendar and wrote an influential work on algebra?

7. Which seventeenth-century mathematician, known as the "father of number theory," proposed a problem that went unsolved for over 300 years?

   a) Fermat   c) Gauss
   b) Foucault   d) Pascal

8. Which Flemish mathematician first converted fractions into the decimal system in 1585?

   a) Leibniz   c) Stevin
   b) Snellius   d) Widmann

9. In a fraction expressed as "b", which number is the denominator and which is the numerator?

10. What is the name of the mathematical tool, originally called "fluxions," that Isaac Newton developed for analyzing the slopes of curves and their adjacent areas?

11. What is defined as "a technique for establishing the distance between any two points, or the relative position of two or more points, by calculations based upon the vertices of a triangle and the length of a side of measurable length"?

12. What is the name for an equation containing a single variable of degree?

13. What word is used to describe an angle of more than 90 degrees but less than 180 degrees?

14. What "value" is equal to the ratio of the circumference of a circle to its diameter?

15. Whose pioneering works on modern symbolic logic during the nineteenth century included the use of binary systems, which are the basis for modern computing systems?
   a) Charles Babbage
   b) George Boole
   c) Leonhard Euler
   d) John Napier

16. How is the value "seven" expressed in the binary number system?

17. Two angles that add up to a total of 90 degrees are said to be what?
   a) complementary
   b) conjugate
   c) supplementary
   d) symbiotic

18. How many sides does a dodecagon have?
   a) 10   c) 12
   b) 11   d) 20

19. What type of triangle has all three sides of different lengths and all three angles of different sizes?

20. What is the sum of all the internal angles of a triangle?

Medicine

1. How did Mary Mallon, a cook working in Oyster Bay in 1903, become famous?

2. What is the leading cause of death in the United States?

3. Which of the following cancers kills the most people each year?

   a) breast
   b) colorectal
   c) lung
   d) prostate

4. What kidney ailment caused the death of President Chester Arthur?

5. What type of human organ transplant is performed most often?

   a) heart
   b) kidney
   c) liver
   d) lung

6. What company manufactures Advil, Anacin and Dristan products?

a) American Home Products
b) Bristol-Myers Squibb
c) Johnson & Johnson
d) Pfizer

7. In what year did Congress approve Medicare?

a) 1934   c) 1954
b) 1944   d) 1964

8. Approximately how many Americans had no health insurance coverage in 2002?

a) Ten million
b) Twenty million
c) Forty million
d) Eighty million

9. Who was the Georgia doctor known for pioneering the use of ether as an anesthesia in 1842?

a) Lyman Hall
b) Henry Grady
c) Crawford Long
d) Joseph Lumpkin

10. What does the acronym "CAT" mean in a CAT scan?

11. In addition to developing the pasteurization process, Louis Pasteur developed a vaccine for which of these?

a) anthrax   c) mustard gas
b) chlorine gas d) smallpox

12. How many people are estimated to have died in the worldwide Spanish flu epidemic of 1918?

  a) Two million   c) Ten million
  b) Five million   d) Twenty million

13. Which is smaller—a bacteria or a virus?

14. Which of these is not a type of bacteria?

  a) Bacilli   c) Spirilla
  b) Cocci   d) Varicella

15. Match the phobia to its fear:

  A. Achulophobia   1. Justice
  B. Batrachophobia   2. Travel
  C. Cynophobia   3. Death
  D. Dikephobia   4. Glass
  E. Ergophobia   5. Vehicles
  F. Hodophobia   6. Drink
  G. Nelophobia   7. Work
  H. Ochophobia   8. Darkness
  I. Potophobia   9. Reptiles
  J. Thanatophobia   10. Dogs

16. True or false? Chickenpox, measles and mumps are all viral infections.

17. What is the name for the sheets of cells that protect sections of the nose, mouth and eyelids, and also protect the digestive and respiratory tracts?

18. What Army surgeon led the Yellow Fever Commission which, in 1901, determined that the disease was spread by mosquitos?

19. Match the medical discovery with the scientist:

A.	Antiseptic surgery	1.	Ehrlich
B.	Aspirin	2.	Pasteur
C.	Blood circulation	3.	Wassermann
D.	Chemotherapy	4.	Lister
E.	Human heart transplant	5.	Gerhardt
F.	Penicillin	6.	Harvey
G.	Rabies vaccine	7.	Barnard
H.	Syphilis test	8.	Fleming

20. In which year did both Salk invent his vaccine for polio and the team of Pincus and Rock invent the birth control pill?

a) 1950   c) 1958

b) 1954   d) 1962

Money

1. Which three European Community Nations had not yet adopted the Euro as their official currency as of 2002?

2. Which island once used stones as large as twelve feet tall as currency?

   a) Easter   c) Hawaii
   b) Galapagos   d) Yap

3. Coins were first used in the kingdom of Lydia, which is found in what modern nation?

   a) Albania   c) Saudi Arabia
   b) Iran   d) Turkey

4. The first use of paper money is credited to what culture?

   a) Chinese   c) Indian
   b) Egyptian   d) Phoenician

5. In 1792 the first U.S. mint was under the responsibility of which government officer?

   a) John Adams
   b) Alexander Hamilton
   c) Thomas Jefferson
   d) Henry Knox

6. What was the name of the solid gold coin of the Byzantine Empire that circulated for almost one thousand years?

   a) Cesterces   c) Justinians
   b) Constantines   d) Solidus

7. Who appears on the gold-colored U.S. one-dollar coins that began production in 2000?

8. Where are the four existing U.S. mints?

9. What three men appear on U.S. currency who were not U.S. presidents?

10. Match these presidents with the denomination of the bills on which they appear:

   A. Jefferson   1. $100,000
   B. Madison   2. $5,000
   C. Jackson   3. $1,000
   D. Grant   4. $500
   E. Cleveland   5. $50
   F. McKinley   6. $20
   G. Wilson   7. $2

11. What was the coin of Venice during the Renaissance?

a) Thaler   c) Florin
b) Dubloon   d) Ducat

12. What is the historic coin of Holland?

13. Name the nine U.S. states that do not tax ordinary income.

14. Name the five U.S. states that do not impose a sales tax.

15. Match the country to its total income and social security tax burden:

A. Australia   1. 7%
B. Canada   2. 20%
C. Denmark   3. 25%
D. Germany   4. 26%
E. Japan   5. 27%
F. New Zealand   6. 33%
G. Turkey   7. 42%
H. USA   8. 43%

16. How many Federal Reserve districts are there in the United States?

a) 8   c) 12
b) 10   d) 15

17. Which of these cities does not have a Federal Reserve bank?

a) St. Louis, MO
b) Kansas City, MO
c) Houston, TX
d) Richmond, VA

18. What is the name of the currency in Croatia?

a) Kuna   c) Hryvnia

b) Schilling   d) Forint

19. Where was the first bank in the United States?

a) Philadelphia, PA

b) Boston, MA

c) Charleston, SC

d) Williamsburg, VA

20. Match the country to its currency prior to the adoption of the Euro:

A. Albania	1.	Markka
B. Angola	2.	Punt
C. Botswana	3.	Zloty
D. Ecuador	4.	Balboa
E. Finland	5.	Lek
F. Haiti	6.	Rand
G. Ireland	7.	Cordobaoro
H. Korea	8.	Kwanza
I. Laos	9.	Baht
J. Lithuania	10.	Pula
K. Nicaragua	11.	Sucre
L. Panama	12.	Gourde
M. Poland	13.	Won
N. South Africa	14.	Litas
O. Thailand	15.	Kip

Mythology

1. What is the name of the Greek goddess of victory whose name endures as a manufacturer of sportswear?

2. What is the name of the Greek god of love known to the Romans as Cupid?

3. Who was it in Greek mythology who fell from heaven after flying too close to the sun?

4. Which food plant was an important motif in Egyptian and Greek stories of the annual cycle of life and death?

   a) corn   c) olives
   b) grapes   d) wheat

5. Mars is the Roman god of War. What is the Greek name for this god?

6. Roman, Greek, Norse and Egyptian mythology each have a figure who is queen of the gods. Which of these goddesses does not belong in this group?

a) Frigg   c) Isis
b) Hera   d) Venus

7. What is the name of the god or goddess of wisdom in each of the following mythologies:

A. Greek
B. Norse
C. Roman

8. Who was the father of Zeus in Greek mythology?

a) Atlas   c) Rhea
b) Cronus   d) Titan

9. Which of these is not a moon god or goddess?

a) Artemis
b) Mama Kilya
c) Njord
d) Thoth

10. What is the name of the eternal location of the ancestral spirits in the mythology of the Australian aborigines?

a) Darktime
b) Dreamtime
c) Startime
d) Suntime

11. In some Native American mythologies, the earth is believed to be balanced on the back of what animal?

    a) buffalo   c) horse
    b) cave bear   d) turtle

12. Match the Babylonian character to his or her role:

    A. Gilgamesh   1. King of the gods
    B. Ishtar   2. Hero
    C. Marduk   3. Sun god
    D. Shamash   4. Moon god
    E. Sin   5. Goddess of love and war

13. What is the name of Thor's hammer in Norse mythology?

    a) Fafnir   c) Skanda
    b) Mjollnir   d) Tyr

14. What is the name of the female Norse spirits who ride horses to carry dead warriors to Valhalla?

15. Who killed the gorgon Medusa?

    a) Ajax   c) Odysseus
    b) Hercules   d) Perseus

16. Odysseus was king of which Greek island?

    a) Crete   c) Iona
    b) Ithaca   d) Malta

17. Who was the father of Hercules?

    a) Apollo   c) Hermes
    b) Ares   d) Zeus

$18.$ How many labors did Hercules have to perform to achieve immortality?

$19.$ Who was the king of Troy?

a) Agamemnon   c) Priam
b) Perseus   d) Priapus

$20.$ Which god did Odysseus anger when he blinded the god's son, the Cyclops?

a) Hephaestus   c) Poseidon
b) Hermes   d) Zeus

The Natural World

1. What is the name of the iron-sulfide mineral commonly called "fool's gold"?

2. Which part of a flower receives the pollen?
   a) anthers
   b) stamen
   c) stigma
   d) style

3. What is the name of the group of plants that includes cacti and uses fleshy leaves or stems to store water?

4. Which of these is not an insect-eating plant?
   a) butterwort
   b) flytrap
   c) pitcher plant
   d) pink medusa

5. What are the three basic types of rocks?

6. Which of these is not one of the five most common elements found within the earth's crust?

   a) aluminum   c) lead
   b) iron   d) silicon

7. Which one hangs from the roof of a cave—stalagmites or stalactites?

8. What is the name of the circular depression formed by the collapse of a volcano's slopes?

   a) caldera   c) crater
   b) core   d) divot

9. What are the three most common components of granite?

10. What is the name of the fossilized resin of extinct cone-bearing trees?

11. Which element is most abundant in the earth's atmosphere?

   a) carbon dioxide
   b) helium
   c) nitrogen
   d) oxygen

12. What is the name of the hard and shiny coal that produces more heat and less smoke than standard types?

13. What is the name of the section of the earth that lies between the crust and its liquid, outer core?

14. True or false? Drills cannot completely penetrate the earth's crust.

15. Which of these countries does not have a large number of active volcanoes?

a) Iceland   c) Japan
b) Indonesia   d) Norway

16. Arrange these oceans in order from largest to smallest:

A. Antarctic
B. Arctic
C. Atlantic
D. Indian

17. Which is greater, the height of Mount Everest or the depth of the Mariana trench in the Pacific Ocean?

18. What is the name of the earth's original single landmass from which the continents drifted beginning 200 million years ago?

19. Since the earth's surface is seventy percent water, the total square miles of land area is approximately how much?

a) 5,700,000   c) 57,000,000
b) 15,700,000   d) 157,000,000

20. Put these geological eras in chronological order:

A. Cenozoic
B. Mesozoic
C. Paleozoic
D. Precambrian

News and Media

1. On what date did Orson Welles broadcast his radio show *War of the Worlds* which caused a panic the next day when it appeared as a newspaper headline?

2. Who was the first U.S. president to address the nation by radio?

   a) Calvin Coolidge   c) Herbert Hoover
   b) Warren Harding   d) William Taft

3. In which city was the United Press founded by the Scripps-McRae League of Newspapers?

   a) Akron, OH   c) Cleveland, OH
   b) Chicago, IL   d) St. Louis, MO

4. Which school of journalism was endowed by Joseph Pulitzer?

   a) Chicago   c) Northwestern
   b) Columbia   d) Syracuse

5. Match the media titan with his company or publication:

A. William S. Paley	1. *Time*
B. Henry Luce	2. NBC
C. DeWitt Wallace	3. AOL
D. David Sarnoff	4. CBS
E. Steve Case	5. ABC
F. Leonard Goldenson	6. *Reader's Digest*

6. In what year did *USA Today* begin publication?

a) 1982   c) 1986
b) 1984   d) 1988

7. What are the call letters of the radio station in Nashville, Tennessee, that broadcasts *The Grand Ole Opry*?

a) WSB   c) WSM
b) WSC   d) WSN

8. In which city was the first U.S. commercial radio station?

a) New York
b) Philadelphia
c) Pittsburgh
d) Washington

9. What newspaper did Adolph Ochs own prior to buying *The New York Times* in 1896?

a) *Chattanooga Times*
b) *Knoxville News-Sentinel*
c) *Memphis Leader*
d) *Nashville Tennessean*

10. Match the historic publisher/editor with his paper:

A. Joseph Pulitzer	1.	*The Liberator*
B. William Randolph Hearst	2.	*New York Sun*
C. James Gordon Bennett	3.	*New York Tribune*
D. Benjamin Day	4.	*New York Journal*
E. William Lloyd Garrison	5.	*New York World*
F. Horace Greeley	6.	*New York Herald*

11. What was the name of William Randolph Hearst's first newspaper?

12. Which New York City newspaper was the first to feature color comics?

13. On April 16, 1912, after playing their first game in the new Fenway Park, the Boston Red Sox did not make the front page of the *Boston Globe* because of what newsworthy event?

14. The Pony Express carried news across the frontier between what two cities?

15. Match the network/cable channel with the year it was founded:

A. CNN	1.	1976
B. ESPN	2.	1979
C. MTV	3.	1980
D. QVC	4.	1981
E. TBS	5.	1982
F. The Weather Channel	6.	1986

16. Which city had the first successful daily newspaper in 1784?

a) Baltimore   c) New York
b) Boston   d) Philadelphia

17. What radio format is the most popular?

a) Country   c) Oldies
b) News/Talk   d) Top 40

18. Which of these is not one of the ten best-selling magazines in the year 2000 based on paid circulation in the United States?

a) *Family Circle*   c) *Time*
b) *People*   d) *Woman's Day*

19. Match the city with its leading newspaper:

A. Austin	1.	*Star-Ledger*
B. Fort Lauderdale	2.	*News & Observer*
C. Little Rock	3.	*Union-Tribune*
D. Louisville	4.	*American-Statesman*
E. Memphis	5.	*Post-Dispatch*
F. Minneapolis	6.	*Mercury News*
G. Newark	7.	*Sun-Sentinel*
H. Pittsburgh	8.	*Courier-Journal*
I. Raleigh	9.	*Democrat-Gazette*
J. St. Louis	10.	*Commercial Appeal*
K. San Diego	11.	*Star Tribune*
L. San Jose	12.	*Post-Gazette*

20. What four U.S. newspapers have a daily circulation of over one million copies?

Poetry

1-10. Identify the poet and poem from the lines shown below:

1. "I wandered lonely as a cloud
That floats on high o'er vales and hills,
When all at once I saw a crowd,
A host, of golden daffodils"

_____

2. "Booth dies blind and still by Faith he trod
Eyes still dazzled by the ways of God!"

_____

3. "Oh, Georgia booze is mighty fine booze,
The best yuh ever poured yuh,
But it eats the soles right offen your shoes,
For Hell's broke loose in Georgia."

_____

4. "Beauty is truth, truth beauty—that is all
Ye know on earth, and all ye need to know."

_____

5. "On the eighteenth of April, in Seventy-five;
   Hardly a man is now alive
   Who remembers that famous day and year."

   ---

6. "Hog Butcher for the World,
   Tool Maker, Stacker of Wheat,
   Player with Railroads and the Nation's Freight Handler"

   ---

7. "There is something about a Martini,
   Ere the dining and dancing begin,
   And to tell you the truth,
   It is not the vermouth—
   I think that perhaps it's the gin."

   ---

8. "On the road to Mandalay,
   Where the flyin'-fishes play,
   An' the dawn comes up like thunder outer China
   'crost the Bay!"

   ---

9. "My apple trees will never get across
   And eat the cones under his pines, I tell him.
   He only says, 'Good fences make good neighbors.'"

   ---

10. "In the middle of the journey of our life
    I came to myself within a dark wood
    Where the straight way was lost."

    ---

11. Name the U.S. poet who made pro-fascist radio broadcasts from Italy and was put into a mental hospital.

12. What poet won the Pulitzer Prize both in 1929 for his epic poem on the Civil War and then again in 1944 for the collection of poems, *Western Star?*

13. Who was the seventh-century Greek poet from the island of Lesbos?

14. What is the name of the collection of poems by Edgar Lee Masters which are set in a small-town graveyard?

15. During the reign of Charles II, who was appointed as the first English poet laureate?

   a) John Dryden
   b) Thomas Mallory
   c) John Milton
   d) Alexander Pope

16. Which of these men was not a Poet Laureate?

   a) W. H. Auden
   b) Ted Hughes
   c) Alfred Lord Tennyson
   d) William Wordsworth

17. Which of these poets won the Pulitzer Prize in 1924, 1931, 1937 and 1943?

   a) Robert Frost
   b) Archibald MacLeish
   c) Edwin Arlington Robinson
   d) Wallace Stevens

18. Who won the Pulitzer Prize in 1923 for *The Ballad of the Harp-Weaver?*

19. What is the name of the epic poem of France that chronicles Charlemagne's campaigns against the Moors?

20. Match the poet to his or her work:

A. W. H. Auden	1. "To His Coy Mistress"
B. William Blake	2. "The Waste Land"
C. Lord Byron	3. "Casey at the Bat"
D. e. e. cummings	4. "Elegy Written in a Country Churchyard"
E. T. S. Eliot	5. "The Rape of the Lock"
F. Thomas Gray	6. "Tulips and Chimneys"
G. John Keats	7. "The Age of Anxiety"
H. Andrew Marvell	8. "Don Juan"
I. Alexander Pope	9. "Songs of Innocence"
J. E. L. Thayer	10. "Ode to a Nightingale"

Politics

1. If the Democratic ticket had won the 1920 presidential election, who would have been the vice president?

2. Who was Thomas Dewey's running mate in 1948?

3. Who was elected president of the first Continental Congress in 1775?
   a) Silas Deane
   b) John Hancock
   c) Henry Laurens
   d) Peyton Randolph

4. Who were the three men who served as vice president under Franklin Roosevelt?

5. Who won over 900,000 votes in the 1920 presidential election while serving time in a federal prison?

6. Which two signers of the Declaration of Independence had sons who grew up to be elected president?

7. Who was the first-ever Republican presidential candidate in 1856?

8. Who was Lincoln's Democratic opponent during his reelection campaign in 1864?
   a) Horace Greeley
   b) George McClellan
   c) Horatio Seymour
   d) Daniel D. Tompkins

9. In what presidential election was the charge of a "corrupt bargain" leveled at the winner?
   a) 1824   c) 1832
   b) 1828   d) 1836

10. What presidential candidate ran on the slogan "Tippecanoe and Tyler, Too"?

11. Which presidential election scandal included the "XYZ Affair"?
    a) 1800   c) 1900
    b) 1840   d) 1916

12. Which man served as speaker of the house for more sessions of Congress than anyone else?
    a) Joe Cannon   c) Thomas "Tip" O'Neill
    b) Henry Clay   d) Sam Rayburn

13. Which U.S. state was the first to give women the right to vote?
    a) California   c) Montana
    b) Colorado   d) Wyoming

14. Name the four main presidential candidates in the election of 1948.

15. What was the name given to pro-secession southern politicians?

    a) Carpetbaggers   c) Fire Eaters

    b) Copperheads   d) Scalawags

16. What third-party presidential candidate won the most electoral votes in a twentieth-century election?

    a) John Anderson   c) Theodore Roosevelt

    b) Ross Perot   d) George Wallace

17. Who was the Democratic candidate in the 1876 presidential election?

18. Who were the four Republican presidential candidates defeated by Franklin D. Roosevelt from 1932 to 1944?

19. Who was Richard Nixon's running mate in the 1960 election?

20. Which of these senators has never been the majority leader?

    a) Howard Baker   c) Bob Dole

    b) Robert Byrd   d) Strom Thurmond

Popular Culture

1. What article of clothing became popular as a result of Fess Parker's role in a Walt Disney television show?

2. What Connecticut company made the tin pie plates that became popular playthings among Yale students?

3. What year did Hula Hoops first become popular?

   a) 1956   c) 1960
   b) 1958   d) 1962

4. What comic book introduced Batman in its twenty-seventh issue in 1939?

5. In which California city did Richard and Maurice McDonald open their first drive-in hamburger restaurant?

   a) San Bernadino   c) San Luis Obispo
   b) San Diego   d) Santa Barbara

6. How many years after the Beatles first visited America was John Lennon killed?

7. What comedy series included skits that featured "two wild and crazy guys"?

8. Which of these events did not take place in 1959?
    a) Death of Buddy Holly
    b) Introduction of the Barbie doll
    c) *Ben-Hur* wins the Best Picture Oscar
    d) Yuri Gagarin's spaceflight

9. In what year did Bob Dylan "shock" the Newport Folk Festival by "going electric"?
    a) 1964   c) 1966
    b) 1965   d) 1967

10. Which of these bands did not play at Woodstock?
    a) Crosby Stills & Nash
    b) Country Joe and the Fish
    c) The Rolling Stones
    d) The Who

11. Which of these individuals was not a member of the Chicago Seven?
    a) Tom Hayden
    b) Abbie Hoffman
    c) Jerry Rubin
    d) Bobby Seale

12. How many people died in the Kent State shooting in 1970?

13.
Huge hype in 1974 led up to Evel Knieval's attempt to jump which river on a rocket-enhanced motorcycle?

a) Colorado   c) Red

b) Columbia   d) Snake

14.
Which of the following Nixon administration officials was not convicted of a Watergate crime?

a) John Ehrlichman

b) H. R. Haldeman

c) John Mitchell

d) Eliot Richardson

15.
In what year did Elvis die, *Star Wars* open and the president pardon the Vietnam-era draft evaders?

a) 1976   c) 1978

b) 1977   d) 1979

16.
Which character from *Dallas* was revealed to have shot J. R. on November 21, 1980?

a) Cliff Barnes

b) Dusty Farlow

c) Kristin Shephard

d) Jenna Wade

17.
With the theme "Energy Turns the World," which city hosted the 1982 World's Fair?

a) Houston, TX

b) Knoxville, TN

c) New Orleans, LA

d) Vancouver, BC

18. In what year did the Berlin wall come down?

19. EPCOT opened at Walt Disney World in 1982. What does the acronym EPCOT stand for?

20. What Irish singer organized the Live Aid concert for famine relief in 1985?

Pop and Country Music

1. Match the country musician with his hit song:

A. Roy Acuff	1. "Ring of Fire"
B. Gene Autry	2. "Your Cheatin' Heart"
C. Garth Brooks	3 "Four Walls"
D. Johnny Cash	4. "Hello Darlin'"
E. Tennessee Ernie Ford	5. "Back in the Saddle Again"
F. Merle Haggard	6. "Wabash Cannon Ball"
G. Jim Reeves	7. "Walking the Floor Over You"
H. Ernest Tubb	8. "Friends in Low Places"
I. Conway Twitty	9. "Okie From Muskogee"
J. Hank Williams	10. "Sixteen Tons"

2. What bandleader created the unique sound known as Texas Swing that was showcased in songs such as "New San Antonio Rose"?

3. What is the name of the Loretta Lynn hit song that was also the title of her autobiography?

4. What singer wrote the hit songs "Eli's Coming," "Stoney End" and "Wedding Bell Blues"?

5. What Bob Dylan album included the songs "Tangled Up in Blue," "A Simple Twist of Fate" and "Lily, Rosemary and the Jack of Hearts"?

6. What musical group sang the songs "The Weight," "Up on Cripple Creek" and "The Night They Drove Old Dixie Down"?

7. Put these hit Beatles songs in chronological order based upon the dates on which they topped the charts:
   A. "Get Back"
   B. "Hard Day's Night"
   C. "Hey Jude"
   D. "Let It Be"
   E. "Penny Lane"
   F. "Yellow Submarine"
   G. "Yesterday"

8. Which Beatles album was the only one to win the Grammy award for album of the year?
   a) *Revolver*
   b) *Sgt. Pepper's Lonely Hearts Club Band*
   c) *Abbey Road*
   d) *Let It Be*

9. Match the singer with the hit song:

A.	Paul Anka	1.	"I'm Sorry"
B.	Frankie Avalon	2.	"Tutti Frutti"
C.	Eddie Cochran	3.	"The Dock of the Bay"
D.	Sam Cooke	4.	"Hello Mary Lou"
E.	Bobby Darin	5.	"Venus"
F.	Fats Domino	6.	"You Send Me"
G.	Brenda Lee	7.	"Runaway"
H.	Little Richard	8.	"Summertime Blues"
I.	Ricky Nelson	9.	"Blue Suede Shoes"
J.	Carl Perkins	10.	"Lonely Boy"
K.	Otis Redding	11.	"Blueberry Hill"
L.	Del Shannon	12.	"Splish Splash"

10. What pioneer of country-rock died in 1973 after a career that included membership in the Byrds, the Flying Burrito Brothers and the Fallen Angels, which featured a young Emmylou Harris?

11. Which of the following record companies was not one of the labels on which Frank Sinatra recorded?

a) Capitol   c) Mercury
b) Columbia   d) Reprise

12. Which two Paul Simon solo albums won album-of-the-year Grammy awards, in 1975 and 1986?

13. Which single won the Grammy for record of the year in 1966?

   a) "California Dreaming"
   b) "Strangers in the Night"
   c) "Tambourine Man"
   d) "Yesterday"

14. Who wrote Patsy Cline's hit song "Crazy"?

15. Which singer never won an album-of-the-year Grammy award?

   a) Judy Garland   c) Barbara Streisand
   b) Carole King   d) Tina Turner

16. Which Bob Dylan album was the first to win the album-of-the-year Grammy?

   a) *Nashville Skyline*
   b) *Planet Waves*
   c) *Slow Train Coming*
   d) *Time Out of Mind*

17. Which group never won an album-of-the-year Grammy award?

   a) The Eagles   c) Steely Dan
   b) Fleetwood Mac   d) U2

18. What 1961 hit song by Henry Mancini was the theme song for the movie *Breakfast at Tiffany's*?

19. Who were the four members of the Monkees?

20. In what city is the Rock and Roll Hall of Fame located?

Presidents

1. Which president published a five-volume *History of the American People* as well as a book on George Washington?

   a) John Quincy Adams
   b) James Garfield
   c) Theodore Roosevelt
   d) Woodrow Wilson

2. Who was the first president to be born a citizen of the United States rather than as a subject of King George?

   a) John Quincy Adams
   b) William Henry Harrison
   c) Andrew Jackson
   d) Martin Van Buren

3. Which president had secret surgery to remove a tumor in his jaw?

   a) Grover Cleveland
   b) Warren Harding
   c) Theodore Roosevelt
   d) Woodrow Wilson

$4.$ Which president was an ordained minister in the Church of the Disciples of Christ?

a) John Quincy Adams
b) James Garfield
c) Warren Harding
d) Benjamin Harrison

$5.$ Match the president with his religious affiliation:

A. William Taft   1. Presbyterian
B. Franklin D. Roosevelt   2. Congregationalist
C. Calvin Coolidge   3. Episcopalian
D. William McKinley   4. Baptist
E. Jimmy Carter   5. Methodist
F. Richard Nixon   6. Unitarian
G. Woodrow Wilson   7. Quaker

$6.$ Two presidents died on July 4, 1826, and one died on July 4, 1831. Who were they?

$7.$ Name the four presidents who were assassinated.

$8.$ Name the four presidents who died in office but were not assassinated.

$9.$ Which former president was later elected to Congress?

$10.$ Name the twelve presidents who have been elected to, and served, two (or more) full terms.

$11.$ Which presidents were elected on the Whig ticket, first in 1840 and then in 1848?

12. The first woman cabinet officer, Frances Perkins, was:

   a) Woodrow Wilson's secretary of the treasury
   b) Herbert Hoover's secretary of the interior
   c) FDR's secretary of labor
   d) Harry S. Truman's secretary of health, education and welfare

13. Match the president with the state in which he was born:

   A. Woodrow Wilson   1. North Carolina
   B. Benjamin Harrison   2. Pennsylvania
   C. Abraham Lincoln   3. Ohio
   D. Millard Fillmore   4. New Hampshire
   E. Dwight Eisenhower   5. Virginia
   F. Calvin Coolidge   6. Texas
   G. Ronald Reagan   7. Illinois
   H. Franklin Pierce   8. New York
   I. James Buchanan   9. Kentucky
   J. James Polk   10. Vermont

14. Which of the following was not one of Martin Van Buren's nicknames:

   a) The Little Magician
   b) Old Kinderhook
   c) The Lost Mohican
   d) The American Talleyrand

15. Who is the only president other than John F. Kennedy to be buried at Arlington National Cemetery?

   a) Warren Harding
   b) Herbert Hoover
   c) Theodore Roosevelt
   d) William Howard Taft

16. Which of the following men was not a presidential assassin:

a) John Wilkes Booth   c) Charles Guiteau
b) Leon Czolgosz   d) Jack Ruby

17. Match the president with his nickname:

A. John Adams   1. Sage of Monticello
B. Andrew Jackson   2. Old Man Eloquent
C. Abraham Lincoln   3. Old Rough and Ready
D. Thomas Jefferson   4. Tippecanoe
E. William Henry Harrison   5. His Rotundity
F. John Quincy Adams   6. Old Hickory
G. Zachary Taylor   7. The Railsplitter
H. Rutherford Hayes   8. His Accidency
I. James Polk   9. Young Hickory
J. John Tyler   10. His Fraudulency

18. In which state were the greatest number of presidents born?

a) Massachusetts   c) Ohio
b) New York   d) Virginia

19. What president, having lost his reelection bid as a Democrat in 1840, ran again as the candidate of the Free Soil Party in 1848?

20. What ex-president ran on the American Party ticket (also known as the "Know Nothings") in 1856?

Religion

1. Approximately how many Americans are Roman Catholics?

   a) Thirty million   c) Fifty million
   b) Forty million   d) Sixty million

2. Rank these American Protestant denominations from largest to smallest based upon number of members:

   A. Baptist
   B. Episcopalian
   C. Lutheran
   D. Methodist
   E. Mormon
   F. Pentecostal
   G. Presbyterian

3. Who became the first American-born saint in 1975?

4. Which Roman Emperor recognized and accepted the Christian faith in A.D. 315?

   a) Constantine   c) Justinian
   b) Diocletian   d) Theodosius

5. Match the individual with the religious organization that he/she founded:

A. John Biddle	1. Christian Revival Association
B. William Booth	2. The Society of Friends
C. Mary Baker Eddy	3. Jehovah's Witnesses
D. George Fox	4. Methodism
E. Ignatius Loyola	5. The Society of Jesus
F. Charles Russell	6. The Latter-Day Saints
G. Joseph Smith	7. Unitarianism
H. John Wesley	8. Christian Science

6. What does the word "Hegira" mean to followers of Islam?

7. What was the first colony to grant religious freedom?

a) Georgia   c) New York
b) Rhode Island   d) Virginia

8. In which state was the Mormon church founded in 1830?

a) Illinois   c) New York
b) Indiana   d) Ohio

9. Which Hindu god is "The Destroyer"?

a) Brahma   c) Shiva
b) Krishna   d) Vishnu

10. In which of these nations is Buddhism not the official state religion?

a) Bhutan   c) Nepal
b) Cambodia   d) Thailand

11. In which of these nations is Islam not the official state religion?

   a) Egypt   c) Pakistan
   b) Jordan   d) Syria

12. Which of these religions did not originate in India?

   a) Sikhism   c) Taoism
   b) Jainism   d) Buddhism

13. Of the four religions listed in question number 12 above, which is the most recent, having been founded during the fifteenth century?

14. Which of the following is not a branch of Buddhism?

   a) Mahayana   c) Therevada
   b) Tantrism   d) Tripitaka

15. What is the dominant branch of Islam that is practiced nine to one over the next-largest segment of the faithful?

16. Which Methodist minister led the "First Great Awakening" in the American colonies during the 1740s?

   a) Jonathan Edwards
   b) Cotton Mather
   c) George Whitfield
   d) Roger Williams

17. What Jewish holiday is the "Day of Atonement"?

   a) Passover   c) Rosh Hashanah
   b) Purim   d) Yom Kippur

18. Which of the names below was never used by a pope?

   a) Cletus
   c) Felix
   b) Fabian
   d) Dominic

19. How many "theses" did Martin Luther post on the church door in 1517?

20. What modern country would include Hippo, the diocese of which Saint Augustine was bishop from 354-430?

   a) Algeria
   c) Scotland
   b) Egypt
   d) Spain

Royalty

1. Whose death in 1066 triggered the invasion of England by William, Duke of Normandy?

   a) Alfred the Great
   b) Canute
   c) Edward the Confessor
   d) Harold

2. What was the name of Henry II's empire, which included a substantial portion of what is now France?

   a) Angevin
   b) Aquitinian
   c) Arthurian
   d) Augustinian

3. In 1166, just 100 years after the Norman Conquest, Henry II was the first king to send English soldiers into which country?

   a) Holland
   b) Ireland
   c) Scotland
   d) Wales

4. Who of the following was not one of Henry II's sons?

   a) Geoffrey
   b) John
   c) Richard
   d) Thomas

5. Which Plantagenet king was nicknamed "Longshanks"? (Hint: He also took the Stone of Scone from Scotland and eventually defeated William Wallace at the Battle of Falkirk in 1298.)

6. Who deposed his cousin in 1399 to become the first Lancastrian king?

    a) Edward the Black Prince   c) Henry Bolingbroke

    b) Edmund Mortimer   d) John of Gaunt

7. What thirteen-year-old prince, together with his younger brother, disappeared in the Tower of London in 1483?

    a) Edward IV   c) Edward VI

    b) Edward V   d) Edward VII

8. What king was the victor in the Battle of Bosworth Field, which ended the War of the Roses?

    a) Henry VI   c) Henry VII

    b) Richard II   d) Richard III

9. Henry VIII, the second son of Henry Tudor, married his dead brother's widow, Catherine of Aragon. What was her first husband's name?

    a) Arthur   c) Hal

    b) Edmund   d) Thomas

10. Match each of Henry VIII's six wives with her eventual fate:

    A. Catherine of Aragon   1. Beheaded in 1536

    B. Catherine Parr   2. Beheaded in 1542

    C. Catherine Howard   3. Marriage annulled in 1533

    D. Anne Boleyn   4. Marriage annulled in 1540

    E. Anne of Cleves   5. Died in childbirth in 1537

    F. Jane Seymour   6. Henry's last wife and widow

11. The first Stuart king, James I, was also King of Scotland where he ruled as:

   a) James IV   c) James VI
   b) James V   d) James VII

12. Which king did William and Mary depose in the "Glorious Revolution" of 1688-1689?

   a) Charles II   c) James II
   b) Charles III d) James III

13. The madness of King George is now attributed to a hereditary illness known as:

   a) hemophilia   c) porphyria
   b) phlebitis   d) schizophrenia

14. Which historical event did not occur during George III's life?

   a) The Fire of London
   b) Captain Cook's first voyage
   c) The French Revolution
   d) The Battle of Waterloo

15. George I spoke no English when he landed on the throne of England in 1714. Where was he born? (Hint: He died there, too.)

   a) Berlin   c) Hanover
   b) The Hague   d) Saxe-Coburg

16. For how many years did Victoria reign after the death of her husband, Prince Albert?

   a) Twenty   c) Forty
   b) Thirty   d) Fifty

17. Who was Victoria in relation to Kaiser Wilhem II of
Germany?

    a) his aunt   c) his grandmother
    b) his cousin   d) his mother-in-law

18. When Edward VII died, which of the following world leaders
was no longer in power?

    a) Czar Nicholas II
    b) Emperor Franz Josef
    c) Kaiser Wilhem II
    d) President Theodore Roosevelt

19. Match the king to his queen:

A. William I	1. Elizabeth of York
B. Henry II	2. Henrietta Maria of France
C. Edward II	3. Charlotte of Mecklenburg
D. Henry VI	4. Alexandra of Denmark
E. Henry VII	5. Margaret of Anjou
F. Charles I	6. Matilda of Flanders
G. George III	7. Eleanor of Aquitaine
H. Edward VII	8. Isabella of France

20. Match the older sibling on the left with his/her younger
sibling on the right (include half brothers/sisters):

A. Richard I	1. James II
B. George IV	2. George VI
C. Charles II	3. Anne
D. William II	4. John
E. Edward IV	5. Elizabeth I
F. Elizabeth I	6. William IV
G. Mary I	7. Richard III
H. Mary II	8. Edward VI
I. Edward VIII	9. Henry I

Science

1. What happens at zero degrees on the Kelvin scale?

2. At which temperature on the Kelvin scale does water boil?

   a) 27   c) 273
   b) 32   d) 373

3. Which of Newton's Laws of Motion states that every action has an equal and opposite reaction?

4. Which European city was the site of the first observatory in 1471?

   a) Cambridge   c) Florence
   b) Cordoba   d) Nuremberg

5. Which of these astronomers discovered the rings of Saturn and the moons of Jupiter?

   a) Nicolas Copernicus
   b) Galileo Galilei
   c) Sir William Herschel
   d) Johannes Kepler

6. Which of these astronomers developed the Laws of Planetary Motion?

   a) Copernicus   c) Halley
   b) Galileo   d) Kepler

7. Which is the branch of zoology involving insects?

   a) ectomology   c) etymology
   b) entomology   d) exomology

8. Who was the Swedish scientist that developed the systems of Taxonomic nomenclature in 1735?

9. What was the name of the ship that took Charles Darwin on his voyage to South America in the 1830s?

10. In which state was Darwin's theory of evolution banned from the public schools, leading to the famous Scopes "Monkey Trial" of 1925?

   a) Alabama   c) Mississippi
   b) Georgia   d) Tennessee

11. Complete this series two places up to the billion level: deci; centi; milli; _____ ; _____ .

12. In what U.S. city did the first sustained nuclear reaction take place in 1942?

   a) Cambridge   c) New York
   b) Chicago   d) Princeton

13. Which of these scientists was not a member of the Manhattan Project team?

    a) Bohr   c) Fermi
    b) Einstein   d) Teller

14. Who was the Austrian monk and botanist whose experiments with pea plants formed the basis of modern genetics?

15. How many sets of chromosomes do human beings have?

16. Who formulated the law of physics stating that the pressure and volume of a gas are inversely proportional?

    a) Robert Boyle
    b) David Brewster
    c) Christian Doppler
    d) Jean Foucault

17. Who was the Russian physiologist that demonstrated the theory of conditioned reflexes in 1914?

18. Which of these is not a particle of matter?

    a) electron   c) neutron
    b) muon   d) photon

19. What scientific team discovered the double helix structure of DNA in 1953?

20. Match the chemical symbol with its element:

A.	Ag	1.	Copper
B.	Au	2.	Potassium
C.	C	3.	Sodium
D.	Co	4.	Nickel
E.	Cu	5.	Silver
F.	Fe	6.	Mercury
G.	Gd	7.	Gadolinium
H.	Hg	8.	Tin
I.	K	9.	Cobalt
J.	Mg	10.	Silicon
K.	Mn	11.	Lead
L.	N	12.	Gold
M.	Na	13.	Iron
N.	Ni	14.	Sulfur
O.	Pb	15.	Carbon
P.	S	16.	Nitrogen
Q.	Si	17.	Manganese
R.	Sn	18.	Magnesium

Space

1. The sun is, on average, 93 million miles from the earth. Approximately how long does it take for sunlight to travel this distance?
   a) Eight seconds
   b) Eighty seconds
   c) Eight minutes
   d) Eighty minutes

2. What is the name for the Southern Hemisphere's equivalent of aurora borealis?

3. What is the seventh planet from the sun?

4. Which planet orbits the sun in the least amount of time?

5. Which two planets in our solar system have no moons?

6. In which year was the planet Pluto confirmed to exist?
   a) 1900
   b) 1910
   c) 1920
   d) 1930

7. What is the mythological name given to Pluto's moon?

    a) Charon   c) Persephone
    b) Pan   d) Styx

8. What planet's moons include Io, Europa and Ganymede?

9. Which of these is not a common configuration of galaxies?

    a) barred spiral   c) elliptical
    b) conical   d) spiral

10. How frequently does Halley's Comet return to the vicinity of the earth?

11. What is the name of the brightest star that is visible from the earth?

12. Which of the following stars is not among the ten brightest as seen from the earth?

    a) Betelgeuse   c) Rigel
    b) Polaris   d) Vega

13. What constellation includes the Big Dipper?

14. Who was the first person to orbit the earth?

15. Which astronaut was the first American to walk in space?

    a) Gordon Cooper   c) James McDivitt
    b) John Glenn   d) Edward White

16. Match the constellation with its mythical image:

A.	Andromeda	1.	Peacock
B.	Aquila	2.	Fly
C.	Cassiopeia	3.	Dove
D.	Cetus	4.	Wolf
E.	Columba	5.	Hare
F.	Cygnus	6.	Eagle
G.	Dorado	7.	Dragon
H.	Draco	8.	Queen
I.	Lepus	9.	Maiden
J.	Lupus	10.	Goldfish
K.	Musca	11.	Whale
L.	Pavo	12.	Swan

17. On what date did Neil Armstrong first set foot on the lunar surface?

18. How many people have walked on the moon?

a) Twelve   c) Sixteen
b) Fourteen   d) Eighteen

19. What are the five names of the space shuttle orbiters?

20. In which year was the first Space Shuttle mission flown?

a) 1979   c) 1983
b) 1981   d) 1985

Spirits, Wine and Beer

1. What is the name of the sweet drink originating in New Orleans that is often cited as the first "cocktail"?

2. What is the name for a spirit that is distilled from wine or fermented fruit juice?

3. In which state did the tax revolt known as the "whiskey rebellion" occur in 1792?

   a) Kentucky
   b) Pennsylvania
   c) Tennessee
   d) Virginia

4. Which state is home to the Jack Daniels distillery?

   a) Kentucky
   b) Tennessee
   c) Virginia
   d) West Virginia

5. Which of these is the critical element of "bourbon whiskey"?

   a) branch water
   b) charred hickory barrels
   c) malted grain
   d) sour mash yeast

6. Which of these grains is not typically used in whiskey distillation?

a) barley   c) oats
b) corn   d) rye

7. In which U.S. presidential administration did the "whisky ring," which involved widespread embezzlement of federal excise taxes by government officials, operate?

a) Grover Cleveland
b) James Garfield
c) Ulysses S. Grant
d) Warren Harding

8. What is the alcohol content of a spirit that is 100 proof?

9. Which of these words refers to a wine connoisseur?

a) oenophile   c) onomatologist
b) ontologist   d) oophyte

10. Which amendment to the constitution was ratified by forty-six states as a result of the Volstead Act?

a) Fourteenth   c) Eighteenth
b) Fifteenth   d) Twenty-first

11. Which of these classic varieties of French grape is not typically associated with the Bordeaux region?

a) cabernet sauvignon
b) chardonnay
c) merlot
d) sauvignon blanc

12. In what country is the Yarra Valley wine region?

13. In which U.S. state was wine first successfully produced from cuttings taken from European vineyards?

   a) California   c) Ohio
   b) New York   d) Virginia

14. In which country would carignan, tempranillo and palomino grapes be used in wine making?

   a) France   c) Spain
   b) Italy   d) United States

15. Which of these is not among the top three wine producing countries?

   a) France   c) Spain
   b) Italy   d) United States

16. Which bottle is larger, a magnum or a jeroboam?

17. Which type of beer uses a cold fermentation process?

   a) ale   c) lager
   b) bitters   d) stout

18. What popular beer is brewed in Latrobe, Pennsylvania?

19. Which of these companies is the world's largest beer brewer?

   a) Anheuser-Busch
   b) Guinness
   c) Heineken
   d) Miller

20. What was produced in the factory Eberhard Anheuser operated in St. Louis before he added a brewery in 1857?

a) carriage equipment
b) pretzels
c) shoes
d) soap

Sports

1. Which two teams competed in the first World Series in 1903?

   a) Chicago and Brooklyn
   b) New York and Philadelphia
   c) Detroit and Cincinnati
   d) Pittsburgh and Boston

2. Which famous pitcher led the Boston Red Sox to the 1918 World Series victory over the Chicago Cubs?

3. What was the name of the first commissioner of baseball, who banned the 1919 "Chicago Black Sox"?

4. Which of these was not among the first five players to be entered in the Baseball Hall of Fame?

   a) Ty Cobb
   b) Christy Mathewson
   c) Babe Ruth
   d) Cy Young

5. Who called for a conference in 1905 to urge a change in college football rules due to frequent player injuries?

6. What four bowl games rotate to host the Bowl Championship Series game?

7. Which Florida city hosts the annual Gator Bowl?
   a) Gainesville   c) Orlando
   b) Jacksonville   d) Tampa

8. Which two schools competed in the first intercollegiate football game in 1869?
   a) Army and Navy
   b) Brown and Columbia
   c) Harvard and Yale
   d) Princeton and Rutgers

9. What is the English translation of the Olympic motto "Citius, Altius, Fortius"?

10. How many gold medals did Mark Spitz win at the Munich Olympic Games?

11. What was the U.S. location for the Winter Olympics in 1932?

12. Where was golf's first U.S. Open held in 1895?
   a) Annapolis, MD   c) Newport, RI
   b) Boston, MA   d) Richmond, VA

13. Match the year of the summer Olympic Games with its host city:

A.	1956	1.	Munich
B.	1960	2.	Atlanta
C.	1964	3.	Moscow
D.	1968	4.	Sydney
E.	1972	5.	Rome
F.	1976	6.	Seoul
G.	1980	7.	Mexico City
H.	1984	8.	Tokyo
I.	1988	9.	Barcelona
J.	1992	10.	Melbourne
K.	1996	11.	Montreal
L.	2000	12.	Los Angeles

14. Which golfer has won the most major professional championships?

a) Walter Hagen   c) Jack Nicklaus
b) Bobby Jones   d) Tiger Woods

15. Which driver is tied with Richard Petty with seven winning NASCAR seasons?

a) Dale Earnhardt   c) Daryl Waltrip
b) Jeff Gordon   d) Cale Yarborough

16. What and where are the three racetracks that host the Triple Crown of horse racing?

17. Which of the following horses did not win the Triple Crown?

a) Man o' War   c) Seattle Slew
b) Omaha   d) War Admiral

18. Which player won the first grand slam in men's tennis in 1938?

   a) Don Budge
   c) Bobby Riggs
   b) Fred Perry
   d) Bill Tilden

19. Which sport was invented at the Holyoke, Massachusetts, YMCA by William Morgan?

   a) Basketball
   c) Racquetball
   b) Ice hockey
   d) Volleyball

20. What sport uses a ball called a "pelota"?

Television

1. Match the actor with his television doctor role:

   A. Adam Arkin   1. Dr. John Carter

   B. Carl Betz   2. Dr. Jack Morrison

   C. Vince Edwards   3. Dr. Marcus Welby

   D. Chad Everett   4. Dr. Joe Early

   E. Gregory Harrison   5. Dr. John McIntyre

   F. David Morse   6. Dr. Ben Casey

   G. Wayne Rogers   7. Dr. Gonzo Gates

   H. Bobby Troup   8. Dr. Aaron Shutt

   I. Noah Wyle   9. Dr. Alex Stone

   J. Robert Young   10. Dr. Joe Gannon

2. Which show replaced *The Smothers Brothers* on the CBS schedule?

   a) *The Carol Burnett Show*

   b) *Hee Haw*

   c) *Rowan and Martin's Laugh-In*

   d) *The Sonny and Cher Show*

3. Who was the president of the United States when *Saturday Night Live* began its first season?

4. Which prime-time series was ranked number one for more seasons than any other show?

a) *All in the Family*   c) *Gunsmoke*
b) *The Cosby Show*   d) *I Love Lucy*

5. Which singer was a guest on Carol Burnett's first show each season?

a) Julie Andrews   c) Jim Nabors
b) Robert Goulet   d) Mel Torme

6. Match the television season with its top rated show:

A. 1955–1956   1. *Wagon Train*
B. 1956–1957   2. *The Cosby Show*
C. 1960–1961   3. *Roseanne*
D. 1961–1962   4. *Happy Days*
E. 1967–1968   5. *I Love Lucy*
F. 1975–1976   6. *All in the Family*
G. 1976–1977   7. *The $64,000 Question*
H. 1987–1988   8. *The Andy Griffith Show*
I. 1989–1990   9. *Gunsmoke*
J. 1990–1991   10. *Cheers*

7. Which of these cable networks is not among the top cable channels based on number of subscribers?

a) Discovery   c) MTV
b) CNN   d) TBS Superstation

8. Which variety show included both Steve Martin and Teri Garr as featured performers?

a) *The Flip Wilson Show*
b) *Rowan and Martin's Laugh-In*
c) *The Smothers Brothers Show*
d) *The Sonny and Cher Show*

9. Which of these reporters was not a *60 Minutes* correspondent?

   a) Dan Rather
   b) Harry Reasoner

   c) Diane Sawyer
   d) Eric Severeid

10. Which former Hollywood star provided the voice of the car on the show *My Mother the Car?*

   a) Joan Blondell
   b) Barbara Stanwyck

   c) Ann Sheridan
   d) Ann Sothern

11. Which of these characters was not one of the original boys on *My Three Sons?*

   a) Chip
   b) Ernie

   c) Mike
   d) Robbie

12. Match the actor with his television lawyer role:

   A. Carl Betz
   B. Raymond Burr
   C. Richard Dysart
   D. Greg German
   E. Steve Harris
   F. Arthur Hill
   G. Burl Ives
   H. E. G. Marshall

   1. Lawrence Preston
   2. Owen Marshall
   3. Walter Nichols
   4. Clinton Judd
   5. Richard Fish
   6. Eugene Young
   7. Leland McKenzie
   8. Perry Mason

13. Which of these situation comedies was set in Boulder, Colorado?

   a) *Family Ties*
   b) *Home Improvement*

   c) *One Day at a Time*
   d) *Mork & Mindy*

14. Who was the host of *To Tell the Truth* during its prime-time run?

a) Bill Cullen   c) John Daly

b) Bud Collyer   d) Allen Ludden

15. Which of these characters is not one of the kids on *South Park*?

a) Benny   c) Kyle

b) Kenny   d) Stan

16. Who played Sgt. Schultz on *Hogan's Heroes*?

a) John Banner   c) Edward Platt

b) Pat Buttram   d) Hayden Rorke

17. Which children's show included the characters Beulah Witch, Colonel Crackie and Fletcher Rabbit?

a) *Beany and Cecil*   c) *Howdy Doody*

b) *Captain Kangaroo*   d) *Kukla, Fran and Ollie*

18. Which actor replaced Joseph Kearns as the character Mr. Wilson on *Dennis the Menace*?

a) William Conrad   c) William Frawley

b) William Demarest   d) Gale Gordon

19. What actress had supporting roles on *The Andy Griffith Show*, *Get A Life!* and *The Odd Couple*?

20. Which of these was not a character created by Red Skelton?

a) Crazy Guggenheim   c) San Fernando Red

b) Freddie the Freeloader   d) Sheriff Deadeye

Theater and Broadway

1. Put these Rodgers and Hammerstein musicals in order from the earliest to the latest:

   A. *Carousel*
   B. *The King and I*
   C. *Oklahoma!*
   D. *South Pacific*

2. Which of these musicals did not feature choreography by Jerome Robbins?

   a) *A Chorus Line*   c) *Gypsy*
   b) *Fiddler on the Roof*   d) *West Side Story*

3. What musical won the Tony over *West Side Story* in 1958?

   a) *Annie Get Your Gun*   c) *Kiss Me, Kate*
   b) *Bells Are Ringing*   d) *The Music Man*

4. Which of these performers was not in the original production of *Bye Bye Birdie*?

   a) Chita Rivera   c) Dick Van Dyke
   b) Dick Gautier   d) Robert Goulet

5. Which of these shows did not star Mary Martin?

a) *Peter Pan*   c) *Damn Yankees*

b) *South Pacific*   d) *The Sound of Music*

6. When *A Chorus Line* swept the 1976 Tony awards, which other notable show did it beat for best musical?

a) *Annie*   c) *Dreamgirls*

b) *Chicago*   d) *The Wiz*

7. Match the musical to the song:

A. *Annie Get Your Gun*   1. "The Best of Times"

B. *Bells Are Ringing*   2. "On the Street Where You Live"

C. *Camelot*   3. "Tradition"

D. *Chicago*   4. "Sit Down, You're Rocking the Boat"

E. *A Chorus Line*   5. "Try to Remember"

F. *The Fantasticks*   6. "'Till There Was You"

G. *Fiddler on the Roof*   7. "Seasons of Love"

H. *Guys and Dolls*   8. "If Ever I Would Leave You"

I. *La Cage Aux Folles*   9. "T&A"

J. *Les Miserables*   10. "All That Jazz"

K. *Man of La Mancha*   11. "There's No Business like Show Business"

L. *The Music Man*   12 "Somewhere"

M. *My Fair Lady*   13. "The Party's Over"

N. *Rent*   14. "The Impossible Dream"

O. *West Side Story*   15. "I Dreamed a Dream"

8. Which Arthur Miller play won both the Pulitzer Prize for drama and the Tony award?

9. Which of these playwrights is a three-time winner of the Pulitzer Prize for drama as well as a Nobel Prize?

a) Arthur Miller   c) Thornton Wilder
b) Eugene O'Neill   d) Tennessee Williams

10. Who wrote the words for Leonard Bernstein's music for *West Side Story?*

11. What 1951 Tennessee Williams play was his only work to win a Tony for best play?

a) *The Rose Tattoo*
b) *A Streetcar Named Desire*
c) *Cat On a Hot Tin Roof*
d) *The Glass Menagerie*

12. In what city did the Rockettes perform prior to their relocation to Radio City Music Hall in New York?

a) Los Angeles   c) Cleveland
b) Chicago   d) St. Louis

13. Which of these won Anthony Shaffer a Tony award for best play?

a) *Amadeus*   c) *A Man For All Seasons*
b) *Equus*   d) *Sleuth*

14. For whom are the annual awards for Off-Broadway productions named?

a) George M. Cohan   c) Roger Bellasco
b) Eugene O'Neill   d) Lucille Lortel

15. What play, later made into a movie with Henry Fonda and James Cagney, won the first Tony awarded for best play in 1948?

16. Match the Stephen Sondheim song with its show:

A. "Barcelona"	1. *Sweeney Todd*
B. "Children Will Listen"	2. *Follies*
C. "Losing My Mind"	3. *Sunday in the Park with George*
D. "Old Friends"	4. *Into the Woods*
E. "Pretty Lady"	5. *Company*
F. "Pretty Women"	6. *A Little Night Music*
G. "Putting It Together"	7. *Merrily We Roll Along*
H. "Remember"	8. *Pacific Overtures*

17. What are the five best musical winners to feature choreography by Bob Fosse, in 1955, 1956, 1959, 1967 and 1999?

18. Which prolific songwriter partnered with Cy Coleman on the music to *Sweet Charity*?

a) Harold Arlen   c) Dorothy Fields

b) Sammy Cahn   d) Oscar Hammerstein

19. Which of these Neil Simon shows won both a Tony for best play and a Pulitzer Prize?

a) *Biloxi Blues*   c) *Lost in Yonkers*

b) *The Odd Couple*   d) *Brighton Beach Memoirs*

20. In which plays did these actors win both a Tony award and later an Academy Award, for the same role?

A. Jack Albertson

B. Anne Bancroft

C. Shirley Booth

D. Jose Ferrer

E. Joel Grey

F. Rex Harrison

G. Paul Scofield

Transportation

1. Which of these ships typically has three masts?

    a) brig   c) schooner
    b) clipper   d) sloop

2. Which was longer, the *Titanic* or the *Hindenburg*?

3. In which year did the Erie Canal open?

    a) 1815   c) 1835
    b) 1825   d) 1845

4. Which railroad line was the first to offer passenger service, beginning in 1829?

    a) B & O   c) Harlem River
    b) Chesapeake   d) Quincy Tramway

5. What railroad tycoon controlled the New York Central Railroad as well as the Hudson River and Harlem Lines?

6. Which railroad entrepreneur helped develop Florida by building lines from St. Augustine to Key West?

a) Francis Dade   c) J. J. Hill

b) Henry Flagler   d) Leland Stanford

7. What was the famous Atchinson, Topeka and Santa Fe train that operated between Chicago and Los Angeles?

a) 20th Century Limited

b) Desert Streak

c) Silver Bullet

d) Super Chief

8. Which of the following was not one of the "Big Four" executives of the Central Pacific Railroad?

a) Charles Crocker   c) Mark Hopkins

b) Doc Durant   d) Collis Huntington

9. Where did the Union Pacific and Central Pacific meet to drive the transcontinental "golden spike"?

10. What was the nickname of Harry Longbaugh, a partner in a Wyoming gang of train robbers?

11. In which town did the Duryea brothers build the first gas-powered motorcar in the U.S.?

a) Buffalo, NY   c) South Bend, IN

b) Rochester, NY   d) Springfield, MA

12. In 1908, who created General Motors by combining the Buick Motor Company with Oldsmobile?

a) David Buick   c) Ransom Olds

b) William Durant   d) Alfred P. Sloan

13. Which automobile company did Walter Chrysler buy in 1925?

a) Dodge Brothers   c) Maxwell
b) Franklin   d) Pierce-Arrow

14. Who designed the first Volkswagen in 1936?

a) Karl Benz   c) Alfred Krupp
b) Walter Gropius   d) Ferdinand Porsche

15. Which automobile company advertised "Ask the man who owns one"?

a) Cadillac   c) Pontiac
b) Packard   d) Studebaker

16. Which family became large shareholders in General Motors after financing its combination with Chevrolet?

a) Astor   c) Rockefeller
b) DuPont   d) Vanderbilt

17. Which company merged with Hudson in 1954 to form the American Motors Corporation?

a) Kaiser   c) Rambler
b) Nash   d) Willys

18. What year did Ford launch the ill-fated Edsel?

a) 1954   c) 1956
b) 1955   d) 1957

19. What type of business did Wilbur and Orville Wright operate when they began their flying experiments?

20. Which airport is the world's busiest based upon annual passenger volume?

a) Atlanta–Hartsfield

c) London–Heathrow

b) Chicago–O'Hare

d) London–Gatwick

U.S. and World Capitals

1. In the lower forty-eight states, what is the northernmost state capital?

   a) Augusta, ME   c) Helena, MT
   b) Bismarck, ND   d) Olympia, WA

2. In the lower forty-eight states, what is the southernmost state capital?

   a) Austin, TX   c) Phoenix, AZ
   b) Baton Rouge, LA   d) Tallahassee, FL

3. What is the latitude of Juneau, Alaska?

   a) 58° N   c) 62° N
   b) 60° N   d) 64° N

4. What is the latitude of Honolulu, Hawaii?

   a) 11° S   c) 11° N
   b) 3° S   d) 21° N

5. Match the European country with its capital:

A.	Albania	1.	Tallinn
B.	Bosnia and Herzegovina	2.	Ljubljana
C.	Bulgaria	3.	Bucharest
D.	Croatia	4.	Bratislava
E.	Estonia	5.	Skopje
F.	Latvia	6.	Vaduz
G.	Liechtenstein	7.	Sarajevo
H.	Lithuania	8.	Tirana
I.	Macedonia	9.	Sofia
J.	Romania	10.	Zagreb
K.	Slovakia	11.	Riga
L.	Slovenia	12.	Vilnius

6. Texas has more counties (254) than any other state. Which state has the second largest number with 159?

a) Georgia   c) Kentucky
b) Illinois   d) Virginia

7. Match the Australian states with their capital cities:

A.	New South Wales	1.	Hobart
B.	Northern Territory	2.	Perth
C.	Queensland	3.	Darwin
D.	South Australia	4.	Sydney
E.	Tasmania	5.	Melbourne
F.	Victoria	6.	Brisbane
G.	Western Australia	7.	Adelaide

8. What African country has a capital named in honor of the fifth American president?

9. Canada's newest territory was created in 1999. Its capital is Iqaluit. What is the name of the territory?

10. What city was Spain's first provincial capital in North America, established in 1565?

    a) Mobile, AL   c) San Antonio, TX

    b) New Orleans, LA   d) St. Augustine, FL

11. Match the Canadian province with its capital:

A. Alberta	1. Regina
B. British Columbia	2. Yellowknife
C. Manitoba	3. Charlottetown
D. New Brunswick	4. Edmonton
E. Newfoundland	5. Whitehorse
F. Northwest Territories	6. Victoria
G. Nova Scotia	7. Toronto
H. Ontario	8. Fredericton
I. Prince Edward Island	9. Quebec City
J. Quebec	10. Winnipeg
K. Saskatchewan	11. Halifax
L. Yukon Territory	12. St. John's

12. Match the African country with its capital:

A. Angola	1. Conakry
B. Botswana	2. Bamako
C. Cameroon	3. Asmara
D. Central African Republic	4. Windhoek
E. Chad	5. Gaborone
F. Eritrea	6. Nouakchott
G. Ghana	7. Luanda
H. Guinea	8. N'Djamena
I. Ivory Coast	9. Yaounde
J. Mali	10. Accra
K. Mauritania	11. Bangui
L. Namibia	12. Abidjan

13. What is the capital of Madagascar?

a) Antananarivo   c) Antseranana
b) Moroni   d) Toamasina

14. Which Asian capital's name means "City of Lions"?

a) Dhaka   c) Singapore
b) Rangoon   d) Tokyo

15. What U.S. state capital has the largest population within its city limits?

a) Austin, TX   c) Columbus, OH
b) Boston, MA   d) Phoenix, AZ

16. What is the capital of American Samoa?

17. What U.S. state capital has the smallest population within its city limits?

a) Augusta, ME   c) Montpelier, VT
b) Juneau, AK   d) Pierre, SD

18. What was the capital of Georgia immediately prior to its move to Atlanta?

a) Macon   c) Savannah
b) Milledgeville   d) Valdosta

19. Which of these European capitals was the first to reach a population of 1,000,000?

a) London   c) Paris
b) Moscow   d) Rome

20. What three cities have served as the capital of Virginia?

World History

1. Which city served as Charlemagne's capital?

   a) Aachen   c) Nuremberg

   b) Avignon   d) Rouen

2. In the year 1000, which of these was the largest city in western Europe, with a population of 500,000?

   a) Cadiz   c) Granada

   b) Cordoba   d) Seville

3. In 1122, which meeting established the supremacy of the pope in appointing bishops, rather than kings?

   a) Council of Nicea   c) Diet of Worms

   b) Council of Trent   d) Fourth Lateran Council

4. Which of these German kings drowned in 1190 while on the third Crusade?

   a) Frederick Barbarossa

   b) Henry V

   c) Ludwig I

   d) Otto the Great

5. In what year did King John sign the Magna Carta at Runnymede?

6. The papal line of demarcation in 1494 divided the territories of the new world between what two countries?

7. In which town did Martin Luther nail his theses to the church door in 1517?

   a) Heidelberg   c) Nuremberg
   b) Konstanz   d) Wittenberg

8. In which year did England execute Charles I and become a commonwealth under Oliver Cromwell?

   a) 1642   c) 1653
   b) 1649   d) 1660

9. The Thirty Years War of 1618–1648 was primarily fought between France and which other power?

   a) England
   b) Holy Roman Empire
   c) Papal and Italian states
   d) Russia

10. How many years was New Amsterdam under Dutch control following its founding in 1626?

   a) Thirty-eight   c) Forty
   b) Thirty-nine   d) Forty-one

11. John Churchill, the first duke of Marlboro, achieved his fame at the Battle of Blenheim during which conflict?

    a) First Anglo-Dutch War
    b) Napoleonic Wars
    c) War of Jenkin's Ear
    d) War of Spanish Succession

12. What is the symbolic date of the beginning of the French Revolution, when the Bastille was stormed?

13. Which former governor of Tennessee became the Republic of Texas' first president in 1836?

    a) Stephen Austin   c) George Dallas
    b) Davy Crockett   d) Sam Houston

14. In which year did the first shipload of English convicts land at Botany Bay in Australia?

    a) 1776   c) 1788
    b) 1783   d) 1800

15. Which of the following was not one of the primary combatant nations during the Crimean War?

    a) Britain   c) Prussia
    b) France   d) Russia

16. What is the name of the legislative body that was created by Czar Nicholas II in 1905 in a step toward the creation of a constitutional monarchy?

17. What war was ended by the Treaty of Portsmouth in 1905?

    a) Boer   c) Franco-Prussian

    b) Crimean   d) Russo-Japanese

18. In which year did the Easter Rebellion occur in Dublin, Ireland?

    a) 1916   c) 1920

    b) 1918   d) 1926

19. Which group did the Nazis blame for the Reichstag fire in 1933?

    a) anarchists   c) Jews

    b) communists   d) republicans

20. Which of these was not among the four essential freedoms expressed by Franklin D. Roosevelt in 1941?

    a) freedom from fear

    b) freedom of religion

    c) freedom of speech

    d) freedom to work

World Leaders

1. In what year was Charlemagne crowned Holy Roman Emperor by Pope Leo III?

2. In 1095, which pope called the Christian Knights of Europe to the first Crusade against the Muslims?

   a) Benedict X   c) Innocent II
   b) Clement III   d) Urban II

3. Which kingdom did Isabella bring to her marriage with Ferdinand II in 1469?

   a) Aragon   c) Castile
   b) Andalusia   d) Granada

4. Which ruler was the sixteenth-century founder of the Mogul empire of northern India?

   a) Akbar   c) Shah Jahan
   b) Babur   d) Tamerlane

5. Who was the Spanish king that launched the Armada against England in 1588, and whose devout Catholicism contributed to the revolt of the Dutch Provinces?

6. Which ruler led the Ottoman Empire to its peak until his death in 1566?

a) Muhammed II   c) Saladin

b) Osman II   d) Suleiman

7. Match the Native American leader to his tribe:

A. Geronimo	1.	Yakima
B. Joseph	2.	Cherokee
C. Kamiakin	3.	Shawnee
D. Little Wolf	4.	Seminole
E. Manulito	5.	Hunkpapa Lakota
F. Metacom	6.	Oglala Lakota
G. Osceola	7.	Nez Percé
H. Pontiac	8.	Navajo
I. Red Cloud	9.	Cheyenne
J. Sequoyah	10.	Apache
K. Sitting Bull	11.	Wampanoag
L. Tecumseh	12.	Ottowa

8. What world leader was born in Corsica in 1769 and died in St. Helena in 1821?

9. Which leader of the 1818 fight to liberate Chile from Spain became its first head of state?

a) Simon Bolivar

b) Benito Juarez

c) Bernardo O'Higgins

d) Jose de San Martin

10. Which nineteenth-century prime minister of Britain supported many popular reforms but lost his leadership position largely as a result of his support for Irish home rule?

    a) Benjamin Disraeli
    b) William Gladstone
    c) Robert Peel
    d) William Pitt (the younger)

11. What British prime minister had, as a young man, written a novel entitled *Vivian Grey* and, in his last decade, entered the upper chamber of Parliament as "Lord Beaconsfield"?

12. What two U.S. presidents won Nobel peace prizes?

13. Which U.S. vice president co-won the Nobel peace prize in 1925 for his plans for German war reparation terms?

    a) Charles Curtis
    b) Charles Dawes
    c) Calvin Coolidge
    d) Charles Fairbanks

14. Which of these Russian leaders was not among the first "troika" within the Politburo following Lenin's incapacitating stroke in 1923?

    a) Lev Kamenev
    b) Joseph Stalin
    c) Leon Trotsky
    d) Grigori Zinoviev

15. What three senators, all of whom later died in office, are the only men to have gone directly from the U.S. Senate to the presidency?

16. Which of these German leaders was known as the "Iron Chancellor"?

a) Otto von Bismarck
b) Paul von Hindenberg
c) Adolph Hitler
d) Arthur Zimmerman

17. Which leader was not present at the 1938 Munich conference where the fate of Czechoslovakia was decided?

a) Edvard Benes
b) Edouard Daladier
c) Adolph Hitler
d) Benito Mussolini

18. Who represented the United Kingdom at the Versailles peace conference?

a) Herbert Asquith
b) Stanley Baldwin
c) David Lloyd George
d) Andrew Bonar Law

19. What New York-born leader of both the Easter Rebellion and Sinn Fein was later prime minister of Ireland from 1932–1948?

20. Where did Winston Churchill, Franklin D. Roosevelt and Joseph Stalin conduct their first joint meeting in 1943?

a) Casablanca   c) Tehran
b) Potsdam   d) Yalta

World War I

1. At the outbreak of World War I, which of these nations was not among the Triple Alliance members?

   a) Austria-Hungary   c) Italy

   b) Germany   d) Spain

2. Which one of the original Triple Alliance members changed sides in 1915?

3. True or false? Japan was allied with Germany during World War I.

4. In which country did the battle of Gallipoli take place?

   a) Bulgaria   c) Italy

   b) Greece   d) Turkey

5. What was the nationality of the famous spy, Mata Hari?

   a) Dutch   c) German

   b) French   d) Polish

6. Which city was the site of the assassination of Archduke Ferdinand, which sparked the beginning of the war?

   a) Belgrade   c) Vienna
   b) Sarajevo   d) Zagreb

7. What was Woodrow Wilson's campaign slogan in 1916?

8. Which country declared war on August 1, 1914?

   a) Austria-Hungary   c) Germany
   b) France   d) Russia

9. Which two nations fought the earliest battles of the war?

   a) Austria and Italy
   b) Austria and Russia
   c) Germany and Britain
   d) Russia and Germany

10. Which Balkan-area nation joined the war against the Allies in October 1914 by bombing Odessa?

   a) Bulgaria   c) Romania
   b) Greece   d) Turkey

11. Who resigned as secretary of state in 1915 because he feared for U.S. entry into the European war?

   a) William Jennings Bryan
   b) John Hay
   c) Herbert Hoover
   d) Robert Lansing

12. What did German Foreign Minister Arthur Zimmermann propose in his infamous telegram?

13. On which date did the United States declare war on Germany?

    a) April 1, 1916   c) April 22, 1917

    b) April 6, 1917   d) April 30, 1917

14. Which of Theodore Roosevelt's four sons was killed in action in a plane over France in 1918?

    a) Archibald   c) Quentin

    b) Kermit   d) Teddy Jr.

15. What significant event led to the decision by Russia to sign the Brest Litovsk treaty in 1918?

16. True or false? The vote on the declaration of war was only one vote short of being unanimous in the House of Representatives.

17. Upon the arrival of his troops in France in 1917, which U.S. officer said "Lafayette, we are here"?

    a) Douglas MacArthur

    b) Billy Mitchell

    c) John Pershing

    d) Charles Stanton

18. What frequent U.S. presidential candidate was sentenced to ten years in prison in 1918 under the Espionage and Sabotage Act for voicing his opinion that industrial workers should not support the war?

19. Approximately how many American soldiers died in World War I?

a) 5,000   c) 250,000
b) 50,000   d) 500,000

20. What is the exact time and date of the armistice that ended the war?

World War II

1. Which country did Italy invade in April 1939?

   a) Albania   c) Ethiopia
   b) Egypt   d) Greece

2. Which nation maintained a neutral position throughout most of the war, though it did send troops to assist in the German assault on the Soviet Union?

   a) Spain   c) Switzerland
   b) Sweden   d) Turkey

3. Which two nations were party to the economic and military alliance known as the "Pact of Steel"?

   a) Britain and France
   b) Germany and Austria
   c) Germany and Italy
   d) Germany and Russia

4. Britain entered the war as a result of the German invasion of which nation?

   a) Belgium   c) France
   b) Czechoslovakia   d) Poland

5. The Allies were forced to evacuate over 340,000 troops at which French port in June 1940?

6. Which of these nations was not fighting against Russia in 1939–1940?

   a) Finland   c) Latvia
   b) Germany   d) Poland

7. Which country did Italy invade in October 1940?

   a) Albania   c) Ethiopia
   b) Egypt   d) Greece

8. True or false? The German assault on the Soviet Union began several months before the United States entered the war.

9. Control of which of these cities was not one of the German objectives in its invasion of the Soviet Union?

   a) Baku   c) Leningrad
   b) Danzig   d) Moscow

10. On what date was Pearl Harbor attacked by Japanese forces?

11. Approximately how many people were killed in the attack on Pearl Harbor?

   a) 400   c) 2,400
   b) 1,400   d) 3,400

12. Who was the American general who led an attack on Tokyo in 1942 with a team of B-25 bombers?

13. What did the acronym W.A.V.E.S. stand for when this noncombat military unit was created in 1942?

14. Which battle was not a success for the Allied forces?

a) Corregidor   c) Guadalcanal
b) El Alamein   d) Midway

15. Which town was the point of landing for one of the two teams of German saboteurs entering the U.S. in 1942?

a) Cohasset, MA
b) Fox Island, WA
c) Groton, CT
d) Ponte Vedra, FL

16. What was the code name for the Allied invasion of France?

17. What was the date of the D-Day invasion?

18. On which beach were the Canadian invasion forces concentrated?

a) Juno   c) Omaha
b) Gold   d) Utah

19. Which 101st Airborne general responded "NUTS" to a German request to surrender at Bastogne?

a) Omar Bradley
b) Benjamin Davis
c) Anthony McAuliffe
d) George Patton

20. Where did the German surrender take place on May 7, 1945?

a) Berlin   c) Rouen
b) Bonn   d) Reims

Answers

American History

1. Illinois, Indiana, Michigan, Minnesota, Ohio, Wisconsin

2. Charlotte, NC

3. d) Tennessee

4. A-7, B-9, C-5, D-2, E-3, F-4, G-1, H-6, I-8

5. 1876

6. Arkansas, Colorado, Iowa, Kansas, Louisiana, Minnesota, Missouri, Montana, Nebraska, North Dakota, Oklahoma, South Dakota, Wyoming

7. c) Chandler

8. d) Weehawken

9. b) Thomas Jefferson

10. John Adams, Benjamin Franklin, Robert Livingston, Roger Sherman

11. a) John Adams

12. b) John C. Calhoun

13. b) John Breckinridge

14. A. October 12, 1492; B. December 26, 1620; C. April 19, 1775; D. October 19, 1781; E. January 8, 1815; F. April 14, 1861; G. April 9, 1865; H. November 11, 1918; I. October 29, 1929; J. December 7, 1941; K. November 22, 1964; L. July 20, 1969

15. b) Nathan Bedford Forrest

16. Jeannette Rankin

17. d) Wampanoags

18. b) Pontiac

19. a) Huron

20. b) Germany

The American Revolution

1. a) Breed's Hill

2. c) 5

3. a) Georgia

4. c) Captured artillery installed on Dorchester Heights

5. A-2, B-5, C-3, D-4, E-7, F-6, G-1, H-8

6. b) Richard Lee

7. Pennsylvania and South Carolina

8. b) Newport, RI

9. a) West Point

10. d) John Andre

11. b) Francis Marion

12. a) British loss at the Battle of Saratoga

13. d) Silas Deane

14. a) 25,000

15. b) Nova Scotia

16. c) Playwright

17. c) Plymouth, MA

18. d) Peyton Randolph

19. False. They served in Connecticut, Massachusetts and Rhode Island.

20. b) Horatio Gates

Ancient History and Civilizations

1. d) West
2. c) Eiffel Tower
3. The Colossus of Rhodes, The Hanging Gardens of Babylon, The Lighthouse of Alexandria, The Mausoleum at Halicarnassus, The Pyramids of Egypt, The Statue of Zeus at Olympia, The Temple of Artemis at Ephesus
4. a) 9
5. b) Howard Carter
6. c) 700
7. d) Persian
8. a) Greek
9. d) Crete
10. d) Fifth century B.C.
11. a) Sparta
12. d) Strategos
13. c) Greeks beat the Persians
14. a) Xerxes
15. D-Socrates, C-Plato, B-Aristotle, A-Diogenes
16. A-4, B-7, C-5, D-9, E-8, F-3, G-6, H-10, I-1, J-2
17. d) 5,000
18. A-3, B-5, C-1, D-6, E-2, F-4
19. B. Julius Caesar, A. Augustus, D. Tiberius, C. Caligula, F. Claudius, E. Nero
20. d) Alaric

Animal Kingdom

1. d) 9,000
2. d) Archaeopteryx
3. a) Mauritius
4. a) .05 oz
5. True
6. d) 98%
7. b) Baboon
8. b) 20,000
9. c) 50
10. b) Anadromous
11. A. Narwhal, B. Sea horse, E. Eel, F. Manta, H. Lamprey, I. Skate, J. Whale shark
1 2. A-3, B-8, C-1, D-6, E-9, F-5, G-4, H-2, I-7, J-10
13. a) Triassic
14. a) Echidnas
15. c) Salamander
16. a) Tuataras
17. b) 900,000
18. D. Fleas, E. Beetles, J. Butterflies
19. a) Termites
20. b) Indian python

Architecture

1. A-7, B-1, C-5, D-3, E-2, F-4, G-8, H-6
2. Atlanta, Houston, Las Vegas, Los Angeles

3. b) Prague

4. a) Anta

5. a) Brooklyn Bridge

6. d) Tacoma Narrows Bridge

7. b) Japan

8. d) Sinan

9. b) Bramante

10. b) Inigo Jones

11. b) Nash

12. A-2, B-3, C-1

13. Gothic

14. d) Plinth

15. b) Le Corbusier

16. a) Gropius

17. d) Weimar

18. d) Wisconsin

19. a) Richard Rogers

20. A-10, B-11, C-1, D-4, E-9, F-7, G-2, H-5, I-12, J-3, K-6, L-8

Art History

1. b) Botticelli

2. d) Paris

3. d) da Vinci

4. c) Flight Into Egypt

5. a) 4

6. c) Raphael

7. C. Renaissance, B. Mannerism, D. Baroque, A. Rococo, E. Pre-Raphaelite, G. Impressionism, F. Fauvism

8. El Greco

9. Jean Honoré Fragonard

10. d) Edward Hopper

11. b) Sir John Everett Millais

12. c) Manet

13. c) Stuart

14. John Trumbull

15. b) 1874

16. B. Monet, C. Pissaro, E. Sisley, F. Cassatt, G. Renoir

17. Georges Seurat

18. James McNeill Whistler

19. c) Klee

20. A-8, B-12, C-13, D-1, E-2, F-10, G-5, H-7, I-4, J-3, K-15, L-14, M-11, N-6, O-9

The Bible

1. a) 39

2. D. Genesis, B. Exodus, A. Leviticus, E. Numbers, C. Deuteronomy

3. c) John Wyclif

4. a) 27

5. d) The Septuagint

6. d) Saint Jerome

7. a) Judith

8. b) Thou shalt not kill.

9. a) Genesis

10. c) 12

11. d) Nimrud

12. a) Nebuchadnezzar

13. b) Ahab

14. d) Esau

15. D. Noah, E. Abraham, H. Isaac, A. Jacob, I. Joseph, B. Moses, J. Joshua, C. Saul, G. David, F. Solomon

16. d) Philistine

17. Seth

18. d) Nod

19. b) Matthew

20. d) Andrew

Business

1. a) 1920

2. d) 1954

3. c) James Landis

4. c) Charles Merrill

5. Thirty

6. d) Bank of America

7. d) Charles Schwab

8. c) J. P. Morgan

9. d) Eugene V. Debs

10. c) 1945

11. a) Buick

12. b) The Buttonwood Agreement

13. d) Philadelphia

14. b) General Electric

15. d) 1972

16. b) 1991

17. Intel, Microsoft

18. c) Pfizer

19. b) Lancaster, PA

20. A-7, B-8, C-6, D-12, E-4, F-10, G-11, H-2, I-5, J-9, K-1, L-3

Children's Literature

1. *The Adventures of Tom Sawyer*

2. c) *Hidden Staircase*

3. A-6, B-3, C-1, D-7, E-2, F-8, G-4, H-5

4. Judy Blume

5. All are Americans.

6. d) Alan Alexander

7. *The Fellowship of the Ring, The Two Towers, The Return of the King*

8. Beverly Cleary

9. F. Jakob Grimm, C. Hans Christian Anderson, A. L. Frank Baum, B. A. A. Milne, E. Dr. Seuss, D. Roald Dahl

10. b) Wobbly Hedgehog

11. c) 7

12. Mycroft

13. d) 20,000 *Leagues Under the Sea*

14. A-4, B-3, C-2, D-1, E-6, F-7, G-5

15. Chris Van Allsburg

16. J. R. R. Tolkien

17. b) Clyde
18. d) The Bubonic Plague
19. Muggles
20. a) *Are You My Mother?*

The Civil War

1. a) Maryland and Pennsylvania
2. d) Martha Washington
3. d) 2,200
4. d) Virginia
5. Tennessee, Texas, Virginia
6. c) Maryland
7. West Virginia
8. Alexander Stephens
9. b) Judah Benjamin
10. b) 365,000
11. a) 75,000
12. b) John Breckinridge
13. c) John Tyler
14. Jefferson Davis
15. c) The Virginia
16. b) Nashville
17. b) Traveler
18. d) Wilmington, NC
19. c) Calhoun
20. c) Edward Everett

Classical Music and Opera

1. b) Saxophone

2. c) New York Philharmonic

3. A. Johann Sebastian Bach (b. 1685), B. Ludwig van Beethoven (b. 1770), D. Richard Strauss (b. 1804), C. Johannes Brahms (b. 1833)

4. b) Allegro

5. Cello, double bass, harp, viola, violin

6. a) 4

7. A-6, B-8, C-1, D-5, E-10, F-9, G-3, H-7, I-4, J-2

8. Aaron Copland

9. Cello

10. b) Oboe

11. Saxophone

12. A-2, B-7, C-8, D-3, E-4, F-1, G-6, H-5

13. d) Leontyne Price

14. Vivaldi, of course!

15. a) John Adams

16. Philip Glass

17. c) La Sonnambula

18. b) Joseph Haydn

19. d) "Pathetique"

20. A-7, B-5, C-6, D-10, E-1, F-2, G-9, H-11, I-4, J-3, K-12, L-8

Computers

1. Universal Automatic Computer
2. d) The Census Bureau
3. b) IBM
4. b) ARPANET
5. .org
6. COmmon Business Oriented Language
7. Beginners All-purpose Symbolic Instruction Code
8. a) 1890
9. c) 1990
10. b) Dell
11. A-6, B-1, C-5, D-3, E-4, F-2
12. HyperText Markup Language
13. Random Access Memory
14. a) 1981
15. b) transistor
16. d) Deep Blue
17. D. IBM, B. Dell, C. Gateway, A. Apple
18. d) Charles Babbage
19. Jim Clark
20. Linux

Film and Hollywood

1. *It Happened One Night, One Flew Over the Cuckoo's Nest, The Silence of the Lambs*
2. c) Laurence Olivier
3. A-4, B-1, C-5, D-2, E-3
4. c) Judy Garland
5. c) Goldfish
6. c) 24 frames/second
7. d) Rudolph Valentino
8. Lighting electrician
9. A-2, B-6, C-4, D-1, E-3, F-5
10. b) The Philadelphia Story
11. Sugar Kane
12. Marnie Nixon
13. a) Flying Down to Rio
14. c) William Wyler
15. Edith Head
16. *Going My Way* won the Best Picture award. Its sequel, *The Bells of St. Mary's*, did not.
17. A-3, B-6, C-2, D-8, E-7, F-5, G-1, H-4
18. A-9, B-8, C-2, D-1, E-7, F-4, G-6, H-10, I-5, J-3
19. A. *West Side Story*, B. *My Fair Lady*, C. *The Sound of Music*, D. *Oliver!*
20. Alfred Hitchcock

First Ladies

1. b) Abigail Adams
2. c) Sarah Polk
3. d) Dolley Madison
4. a) Edith Roosevelt
5. b) Abigail Adams
6. d) Elizabeth Monroe
7. a) Louisa Adams
8. Anna Harrison
9. c) Ida McKinley
10. c) Anna Harrison
11. d) Abigail Fillmore
12. Lucy Hayes
13. A-4, B-8, C-9, D-2, E-10, F-3, G-5, H-1, I-6, J-7
14. a) Frances Cleveland
15. a) Ida McKinley
16. a) Frances Cleveland
17. a) Edith Roosevelt
18. d) Lucy Hayes
19. b) Jacqueline Bouvier
20. a) Jacqueline Kennedy

Food

1. c) Pepsi-Cola
2. b) Olive oil

3. Cold pressing—no heat is used.

4. a) Ketchup

5. b) Blanching

6. Cream of tartar

7. a) Amberjack

8. b) Gorgonzola

9. Sixteen

10. a) Herbs

11. Squash

12. d) Theodore Roosevelt

13. c) Ice-cream cones

14. Waldorf salad

15. a) Arby's

16. chick peas (garbanzo beans)

17. b) Marjoram

18. d) Ragout

19. a) Mexico

20. b) Jif

Games and Toys

1. c) Baccarat

2. Badminton

3. c) 50

4. B&O, Pennsylvania, Reading, Short Line

5. d) St. Charles Place

6. a) Pinochle

7. b) Playskool

8. c) 00

9. Full house, four of a kind

10. d) 7 or 11

11. d) Tripella

12. A jackknife

13. d) Frank Lloyd Wright

14. Mr. Green, Colonel Mustard, Mrs. Peacock, Professor Plum, Miss Scarlet, Mrs. White

15. Takes a hit

16. b) 3

17. None

18. a) Flunk

19. a) Denmark

20. Bishop, King, Knight, Pawn, Queen, Rook (Castle)

Geography

1. A. Charleston, SC, C. Charlotte, NC, F. Columbia, SC, B. Charleston, WV, E. Cleveland, OH, H. Columbus, OH, G. Columbus, GA, D. Chattanooga, TN

2. E. Nashville, TN, G. Raleigh, NC, C. Los Angeles, CA, A. Atlanta, GA, B. Jackson, MI, D. Mobile, AL, H. San Antonio, TX, F. Orlando, FL

3. b) Greenland

4. d) Lisbon, Portugal

5. Missouri, Tennessee

6. Arizona, Colorado, New Mexico, Utah

7. b) Illinois

8. True

9. Maine

10. a) Alaska

11. c) New Guinea

12. B. Berlin, Germany, C. London, England, G. Toronto, Canada, H. Washington, DC, A. Athens, Greece, F. Tokyo, Japan, E. New Delhi, India, D. Mexico City, Mexico

13. d) China

14. Eleven

15. Vatican City

16. b) Honshu

17. A-5, B-10, C-6, D-8, E-4, F-1, G-7, H-9, I-2, J-3

18. b) Jacksonville, FL

19. b) Borneo

20. a) Blarney

Government

1. d) Switzerland

2. b) 189

3. d) San Francisco

4. c) Dean Rusk

5. China, France, Russia, United Kingdom, United States

6. Belgium, France, Germany, Italy, Luxembourg, The Netherlands

7. c) Norway

8. d) Thailand

9. Balearics

10. d) 54

11. b) Franklin Roosevelt

12. d) William Rogers

13. d) Christine Todd Whitman

14. b) Barbados

15. d) Portugal

16. A. Chin, D. Yuan, B. Ming, C. Qing

17. b) 30

18. James K. Polk

19. a) Bourbon

20. b) Georgia

Higher Education

1. c) 1802

2. c) New London, CT

3. c) Cotton Mather

4. d) Oberlin

5. b) Indiana

6. c) Missouri

7. University of Georgia

8. b) 86,000

9. a) Bologna

10. d) United States

11. King's College

12. b) Florida State

13. c) Duke

14. Columbia

15. Princeton (Woodrow Wilson) and Columbia (Dwight D. Eisenhower)

16. a) Georgia
17. Doctor of Divinity
18. b) Michigan
19. d) Richard Nixon
20. A-10, B-8, C-3, D-2, E-4, F-11, G-5, H-6, I-12, J-1, K-9, L-7

Human Body

1. 206
2. c) 350
3. d) stirrup
4. Skull
5. b) Thoracic
6. A-5, B-7, C-1, D-3, E-4, F-6, G-8, H-2
7. b) Pituitary
8. Kidneys
9. a) Patellas
10. O
11. AB
12. b) 77
13. Lungs
14. Meiosis
15. Muscles
16. Teeth
17. Black bile, yellow bile, blood, phlegm
18. Right
19. Cerebral cortex
20. d) Delta

Inventions

1. a) Copper and tin
2. b) 1447
3. d) Lewis Waterman
4. a) Savannah
5. d) Volvo
6. False
7. b) 1793
8. d) Electric battery
9. c) Wilhelm Conrad Roentgen
10. a) Painter
11. c) Alternating-current motor
12. Sweden
13. b) John Harrison
14. Harmonica
15. The Otis elevator
16. b) 90 minutes (Before 1913 it took more than twelve hours to build a Model T.)
17. Thomas Edison
18. d) Billiard balls
19. b) Hot air balloon
20. a) Dunlop

Jazz

1. d) "I've Got My Love to Keep Me Warm"
2. a) Count Basie

3. d) Dorothy Fields

4. "Strange Fruit"

5. a) Cole Porter

6. d) Indiana

7. b) Benny Goodman

8. a) Hoagy Carmichael

9. b) Billie Holiday

10. c) Louis Prima

11. Tommy Dorsey

12. Django Reinhardt

13. Mel Torme

14. a) Original Dixieland Jazz Band

15. c) King Oliver

16. d) Piano

17. Edward Kennedy Ellington

18. a) Chick Webb

19. Piano

20. A-5, B-6, C-1, D-7, E-8, F-4, G-3, H-2

Language

1. A. civic, B. kayak, C. madam, D. shahs, E. solos

2. c) Philippines

3. b) French

4. a) India

5. Maine

6. Port Out Starboard Home

7. Bar tabs—"pints and quarts"

8. E,T,A

9. "The," "And," "I"

10. A-5, B-6, C-7, D-8, E-3, F-9, G-10, H-4, I-2, J-1

11. echo, foxtrot, golf, hotel

12. Flemish, French

13. Brazil

14. French, German, Italian, Romansch

15. A-5, B-3, C-1, D-2, E-4

16. A word that is spelled the same way as another but pronounced differently. For example, "bow" as in arrow, and "bow" as in to bend at the waist.

17. Seqoyah

18. d) Tibetan

19. d) 1833

20. Diphthong

Law

1. c) Robert Jackson

2. a) Hermann Goering

3. a) Hugo Black

4. Charles E. Hughes

5. b) Henry II

6. John Adams

7. Clarence Darrow

8. b) William O. Douglas

9. c) 70

10. Lance Ito
11. d) Virginia
12. a) Harry Blackmun
13. a) 27
14. b) John Jay
15. b) Nebraska
16. Tort
17. The right to bear arms
18. Marbury v. Madison
19. Thurgood Marshall
20. True

Literature and Shakespeare

1. *The Taming of the Shrew*
2. *A Midsummer Night's Dream*
3. *Hamlet*
4. *Julius Caesar*
5. *Henry VI Part Two*
6. d) Portia
7. *King Lear*
8. O. Henry
9. A-10, B-6, C-7, D-11, E-1, F-8, G-4, H-2, I-5, J-12, K-3, L-9
10. c) Patience and Fortitude
11. *The Metamorphosis*
12. a) Sinclair Lewis
13. d) *The Lost Generation*

14. Buck

15. b) Toni Morrison

16. Joad

17. c) *The Pickwick Papers*

18. Friedrich Engels

19. b) Nick Carraway

20. b) *There's One Born Every Minute*

Mathematics

1. Pythagoras

2. Euclid

3. a) Archimedes

4. c) Hindu

5. CCLXXXVIII

6. Omar Khayyam

7. a) Fermat

8. c) Stevin

9. 2 is the numerator, 3 is the denominator.

10. Calculus

11. Triangulation

12. Quadratic

13. Obtuse

14. Pi (3.14 . . .)

15. b) George Boole

16. 111

17. a) complementary

18. c) 12
19. Scalene
20. 180 degrees

Medicine

1. "Typhoid Mary" spread the infectious disease.
2. Heart disease
3. c) lung
4. Bright's disease
5. b) kidney
6. a) American Home Products
7. d) 1964
8. c) 40 million
9. c) Crawford Long
10. Computerized Axial Tomography
11. a) anthrax
12. d) Twenty million
13. A virus
14. d) Varicella
15. A-8, B-9, C-10, D-1, E-7, F-2, G-4, H-5, I-6, J-3
16. True
17. Mucous membranes
18. Walter Reed
19. A-4, B-5, C-6, D-1, E-7, F-8, G-2, H-3
20. b) 1954

Money

1. Denmark, Sweden, United Kingdom
2. d) Yap
3. d) Turkey
4. a) Chinese
5. c) Thomas Jefferson
6. d) Solidus
7. Sacagawea
8. Denver, CO, Philadelphia, PA, San Francisco, CA, West Point, NY
9. Salmon Chase, Benjamin Franklin, Alexander Hamilton
10. A-7, B-2, C-6, D-5, E-3, F-4, G-1
11. d) Ducat
12. Guilder
13. Alaska, Florida, Nevada, New Hampshire, South Dakota, Tennessee, Texas, Washington, Wyoming
14. Alaska, Delaware, Montana, New Hampshire, Oregon
15. A-3, B-5, C-8, D-7, E-1, F-2, G-6, H-4
16. c) 12
17. c) Houston, TX
18. a) Kuna
19. a) Philadelphia, PA
20. A-5, B-8, C-10, D-11, E-1, F-12, G-2, H-13, I-15, J-14, K-7, L-4, M-3, N-6, O-9

Mythology

1. Nike
2. Eros
3. Icarus
4. a) corn
5. Ares
6. d) Venus
7. A. Athena, B. Mimir, C. Minerva
8. b) Cronus
9. c) Njord
10. b) Dreamtime
11. d) turtle
12. A-2, B-5, C-1, D-3, E-4
13. b) Mjollnir
14. Valkyries
15. d) Perseus
16. b) Ithaca
17. d) Zeus
18. Twelve
19. c) Priam
20. c) Poseidon

The Natural World

1. Pyrite
2. c) stigma

3. Succulents

4. d) pink medusa

5. Igneous, metamorphic, sedimentary

6. c) lead

7. stalactites

8. a) caldera

9. Feldspar, mica, quartz

10. Amber

11. c) nitrogen

12. Anthracite

13. Mantle

14. True

15. d) Norway

16. C, D, A, B

17. Mariana trench

18. Pangaea

19. c) 57,000,000

20. D. Precambrian, C. Paleozoic, B. Mesozoic, A. Cenozoic

News and Media

1. October 31, 1938

2. a) Calvin Coolidge

3. c) Cleveland

4. b) Columbia

5. A-4, B-1, C-6, D-2, E-3, F-5

6. a) 1982

7. c) WSM

8. c) Pittsburgh

9. a) *Chattanooga Times*

10. A-5, B-4, C-6, D-2, E-1, F-3

11. *San Francisco Examiner*

12. *New York World*

13. The sinking of the Titanic

14. St. Joseph, Missouri, and Sacramento, California

15. A-3, B-2, C-4, D-6, E-1, F-5

16. d) Philadelphia

17. a) Country

18. b) *People*

19. A-4, B-7, C-9, D-8, E-10, F-11, G-1, H-12, I-2, J-5, K-3, L-6

20. *Los Angeles Times, The New York Times, USA Today, Wall Street Journal*

Poetry

1. William Wordsworth, "I Wandered Lonely as a Cloud"

2. Vachel Lindsay, "General William Booth Enters Into Heaven"

3. Stephen Vincent Benet, "Mountain Whippoorwill"

4. John Keats, "Ode on a Grecian Urn"

5. Henry Wadsworth Longfellow, "Paul Revere's Ride"

6. Carl Sandburg, "Chicago"

7. Ogden Nash, "A Drink with Something in It"

8. Rudyard Kipling, "Mandalay"

9. Robert Frost, "Mending Wall"

10. Dante Alighieri, Canto I., vv. 1-6, Inferno

11. Ezra Pound

12. Stephen Vincent Benet

13. Sappho

14. *Spoon River Anthology*

15. a) John Dryden

16. a) W. H. Auden

17. a) Robert Frost

18. Edna St. Vincent Millay

19. "Song of Roland"

20. A-7, B-9, C-8, D-6, E-2, F-4, G-10, H-1, I-5, J-3

Politics

1. Franklin D. Roosevelt

2. Earl Warren

3. d) Peyton Randolph

4. John Nance Garner, Harry Truman, Henry Wallace

5. Eugene V. Debs

6. John Adams and Benjamin Harrison

7. John C. Fremont

8. b) George McClellan

9. a) 1824

10. William Henry Harrison

11. a) 1800

12. d) Sam Rayburn

13. d) Wyoming

14. Thomas Dewey, Strom Thurmond, Harry Truman, Henry Wallace

15. c) Fire Eaters

16. c) Theodore Roosevelt

17. Samuel J. Tilden

18. Herbert Hoover, Alf Landon, Wendell Willkie, Thomas Dewey

19. Henry Cabot Lodge

20. d) Strom Thurmond

Pop Culture

1. Coonskin caps

2. Frisbie Baking Company

3. b) 1958

4. Detective Comics

5. a) San Bernadino

6. Sixteen

7. *Saturday Night Live*

8. d) Yuri Gagarin's spaceflight

9. b) 1965

10. c) The Rolling Stones

11. d) Bobby Seale

12. Four

13. d) Snake

14. d) Eliot Richardson

15. b) 1977

16. c) Kristin Shephard

17. b) Knoxville, TN

18. 1989

19. Experimental Prototype Community Of Tomorrow
20. Bob Geldof

Pop Music

1. A-6, B-5, C-8, D-1, E-10, F-9, G-3, H-7, I-4, J-2
2. Bob Wills
3. "Coal Miner's Daughter"
4. Laura Nyro
5. *Blood on the Tracks*
6. The Band
7. B. "Hard Day's Night," G. "Yesterday," F. "Yellow Submarine," E. "Penny Lane," C. "Hey Jude," A. "Get Back," D. "Let It Be"
8. b) *Sgt. Pepper's Lonely Hearts Club Band*
9. A-10, B-5, C-8, D-6, E-12, F-11, G-1, H-2, I-4, J-9, K-3, L-7
10. Gram Parsons
11. c) Mercury
12. *Still Crazy After All These Years* and *Graceland*
13. b) "Strangers in the Night"
14. Willie Nelson
15. d) Tina Turner
16. d) *Time Out of Mind*
17. a) The Eagles
18. "Moon River"
19. Micky Dolenz, Davy Jones, Mike Nesmith, Peter Tork
20. Cleveland, Ohio

Presidents

1. d) Woodrow Wilson

2. d) Martin Van Buren

3. a) Grover Cleveland

4. b) James Garfield

5. A-6, B-3, C-2, D-5, E-4, F-7, G-1

6. John Adams and Thomas Jefferson died on July 4, 1826. James Monroe died on July 4, 1831.

7. Abraham Lincoln, James Garfield, William McKinley, John F. Kennedy

8. William Henry Harrison, Zachary Taylor, Warren G. Harding, Franklin D. Roosevelt

9. John Quincy Adams

10. George Washington, Thomas Jefferson, James Madison, James Monroe, Andrew Jackson, Ulysses S. Grant, Grover Cleveland, Woodrow Wilson, Franklin D. Roosevelt, Dwight Eisenhower, Ronald Reagan, Bill Clinton

11. William Henry Harrison and Zachary Taylor

12. c) FDR's secretary of labor

13. A-5, B-3, C-9, D-8, E-6, F-10, G-7, H-4, I-2, J-1

14. c) The Lost Mohican

15. d) William Howard Taft

16. d) Jack Ruby

17. A-5, B-6, C-7, D-1, E-4, F-2, G-3, H-10, I-9, J-8

18. d) Virginia

19. Martin Van Buren

20. Millard Fillmore

Religion

1. d) Sixty million
2. A. Baptist, D. Methodist, F. Pentecostal, C. Lutheran, E. Mormon, G. Presbyterian, B. Episcopalian
3. Elizabeth Anne Seton
4. a) Constantine
5. A-7, B-1, C-8, D-2, E-5, F-3, G-6, H-4
6. Flight or journey
7. b) Rhode Island
8. c) New York
9. c) Shiva
10. c) Nepal
11. d) Syria
12. c) Taoism
13. Sikhism
14. d) Tripitaka
15. Sunni
16. c) George Whitfield
17. d) Yom Kippur
18. d) Dominic
19. Ninety-five
20. a) Algeria

Royalty

1. c) Edward the Confessor
2. a) Angevin

3. b) Ireland

4. d) Thomas

5. Edward II

6. c) Henry Bolingbroke

7. b) Edward V

8. c) Henry VII

9. a) Arthur

10. A-3, B-6, C-2, D-1, E-4, F-5

11. c) James VI

12. c) James II

13. c) porphyria

14. a) The Fire of London

15. c) Hanover

16. c) Forty

17. c) his grandmother

18. d) President Theodore Roosevelt

19. A-6, B-7, C-8, D-5, E-1, F-2, G-3, H-4

20. A-4, B-6, C-1, D-9, E-7, F-8, G-5 and 8, H-3, I-2

Science

1. At absolute zero, molecular motion stops.

2. d) 373

3. Third

4. d) Nuremberg

5. b) Galileo Galilei

6. d) Kepler

7. b) entomology

8. Carl Linnaeus

9. H.M.S. *Beagle*

10. d) Tennessee

11. micro, nano

12. b) Chicago

13. b) Einstein

14. Gregor Mendel

15. Forty-six

16. a) Robert Boyle

17. Ivan Pavlov

18. d) photon

19. James Watson and Francis Crick

20. A-5, B-12, C-15, D-9, E-1, F-13, G-7, H-6, I-2, J-18, K-17, L-16, M-3, N-4, O-11, P-14, Q-10, R-8

Space

1. c) Eight minutes

2. aurora australis

3. Uranus

4. Mercury, in 88 days.

5. Mercury and Venus

6. d) 1930

7. a) Charon

8. Jupiter

9. c) elliptical

10. Every 76 years

11. Sirius, the dog star, also known as Canis Major
12. b) Polaris
13. Ursa Major, the big bear
14. Yuri Gagarin
15. d) Edward White
16. A-9, B-6, C-8, D-11, E-3, F-12, G-10, H-7, I-5, J-4, K-2, L-1
17. July 20, 1969
18. a) Twelve
19. Atlantis, Challenger, Columbia, Discovery, Endeavour
20. b) 1981

Spirits, Wine and Beer

1. Sazerac
2. Brandy
3. b) Pennsylvania
4. b) Tennessee
5. d) sour mash yeast
6. c) oats
7. c) Ulysses S. Grant
8. 50%
9. a) oenophile
10. c) Eighteenth
11. b) chardonnay
12. Australia
13. a) California
14. c) Spain

15. d) United States
16. Jeroboam
17. c) lager
18. Rolling Rock
19. a) Anheuser-Busch
20. d) soap

Sports

1. d) Pittsburgh and Boston
2. Babe Ruth
3. Kenesaw Mountain Landis
4. d) Cy Young
5. Theodore Roosevelt
6. Fiesta, Orange, Rose, Sugar
7. b) Jacksonville
8. d) Princeton and Rutgers
9. Swifter, Higher, Stronger
10. Seven
11. Lake Placid, New York
12. c) Newport, RI
13. A-10, B-5, C-8, D-7, E-1, F-11, G-3, H-12, I-6, J-9, K-2, L-4
14. c) Jack Nicklaus
15. a) Dale Earnhardt
16. Kentucky Derby at Churchill Downs in Louisville, Kentucky, Belmont Stakes at Belmont Park, Long Island, Preakness Stakes at Pimlico Race Course in Baltimore, Maryland
17. a) Man o' War

18. a) Don Budge
19. d) Volleyball
20. Jai alai

Television

1. A-8, B-9, C-6, D-10, E-7, F-2, G-5, H-4, I-1, J-3
2. b) *Hee Haw*
3. Gerald Ford
4. a) *All in the Family*
5. c) Jim Nabors
6. A-7, B-5, C-9, D-1, E-8, F-6, G-4, H-2, I-3, J-10
7. c) MTV
8. d) *The Sonny and Cher Show*
9. d) Eric Severeid
10. d) Ann Sothern
11. b) Ernie
12. A-4, B-8, C-7, D-5, E-6, F-2, G-3, H-1
13. d) *Mork & Mindy*
14. b) Bud Collyer
15. a) Benny
16. a) John Banner
17. d) *Kukla, Fran and Ollie*
18. d) Gale Gordon
19. Elinor Donahue
20. a) Crazy Guggenheim

Theater and Broadway

1. C. *Oklahoma*, A. *Carousel*, D. *South Pacific*, B. *The King and I*

2. a) *A Chorus Line*

3. d) *The Music Man*

4. d) Robert Goulet

5. c) *Damn Yankees*

6. b) *Chicago*

7. A-11, B-13, C-8, D-10, E-9, F-5, G-3, H-4, I-1, J-15, K-14, L-6, M-2, N-7, O-12

8. *Death of a Salesman*

9. b) Eugene O'Neill

10. Stephen Sondheim

11. a) *The Rose Tattoo*

12. d) St. Louis

13. d) *Sleuth*

14. d) Lucille Lortel

15. *Mr. Roberts*

16. A-5, B-4, C-2, D-7, E-8, F-1, G-3, H-6

17. *Pajama Game, Damn Yankees, Redhead, Cabaret, Fosse*

18. c) Dorothy Fields

19. c) Lost in Yonkers

20. A. *The Subject Was Roses*

    B. *The Miracle Worker*

    C. *Come Back, Little Sheba*

    D. *Cyrano*

    E. *Cabaret*

    F. *My Fair Lady*

    G. *A Man for All Seasons*

Transportation

1. b) clipper
2. The *Titanic*, by 83 feet
3. b) 1825
4. a) B & O
5. Cornelius Vanderbilt
6. b) Henry Flagler
7. d) Super Chief
8. b) Doc Durant
9. Promontory Point, Utah
10. The Sundance Kid
11. d) Springfield, MA
12. b) William Durant
13. c) Maxwell
14. d) Ferdinand Porsche
15. b) Packard
16. b) DuPont
17. b) Nash
18. d) 1957
19. A bicycle shop
20. a) Atlanta–Hartsfield

U.S. and World Capitals

1. d) Olympia, WA
2. a) Austin, TX

3. a) 58° N
4. d) 21° N
5. A-8, B-7, C-9, D-10, E-1, F-11, G-6, H-12, I-5, J-3, K-4, L-2
6. a) Georgia
7. A-4, B-3, C-6, D-7, E-1, F-5, G-2
8. Monrovia, Liberia
9. Nunavut
10. d) St. Augustine, FL
11. A-4, B-6, C-10, D-8, E-12, F-2, G-11, H-7, I-3, J-9, K-1, L-5
12. A-7, B-5, C-9, D-11, E-8, F-3, G-10, H-1, I-12, J-2, K-6, L-4
13. a) Antananarivo
14. c) Singapore
15. d) Phoenix, AZ
16. Pago Pago
17. c) Montpelier, VT
18. b) Milledgeville
19. d) Rome
20. Jamestown, Williamsburg, Richmond

World History

1. a) Aachen
2. b) Cordoba
3. c) Diet of Worms
4. a) Frederick Barbarossa
5. 1215
6. Portugal and Spain
7. d) Wittenberg

8. a) 1642

9. b) Holy Roman Empire

10. a) Thirty-eight

11. d) War of Spanish Succession

12. July 14, 1789

13. d) Sam Houston

14. c) 1788

15. c) Prussia

16. Duma

17. d) Russo-Japanese

18. a) 1916

19. b) communists

20. d) freedom to work

World Leaders

1. 800

2. d) Urban II

3. c) Castile

4. b) Babur

5. Philip II

6. d) Suleiman

7. A-10, B-7, C-1, D-9, E-8, F-11, G-4, H-12, I-6, J-2, K-5, L-3

8. Napoleon Bonaparte

9. c) Bernardo O'Higgins

10. b) William Gladstone

11. Benjamin Disraeli

12. Theodore Roosevelt and Woodrow Wilson

13. b) Charles Dawes

14. c) Leon Trotsky

15. James Garfield, Warren Harding, John F. Kennedy

16. a) Otto von Bismarck

17. a) Edvard Benes

18. c) David Lloyd George

19. Eamon de Valera

20. c) Tehran

World War I

1. d) Spain

2. Italy

3. False

4. d) Turkey

5. a) Dutch

6. b) Sarajevo

7. He kept us out of war.

8. c) Germany

9. d) Russia and Germany

10. d) Turkey

11. a) William Jennings Bryan

12. An attack on the United States by Mexico

13. b) April 6, 1917

14. c) Quentin

15. The Russian Revolution in October/November 1917

16. False. There were fifty votes against entry into the war.
17. d) Charles Stanton
18. Eugene V. Debs
19. b) 50,000
20. November 11, 1918 at 11:00 A.M.

World War II

1. a) Albania
2. a) Spain
3. c) Germany and Italy
4. d) Poland
5. Dunkirk
6. b) Germany
7. d) Greece
8. True. It began in June 1941.
9. b) Danzig
10. December 7, 1941
11. c) 2,400
12. James Doolittle
13. Women Accepted for Voluntary Emergency Service
14. a) Corregidor
15. d) Ponte Vedra, FL
16. Operation Overlord
17. June 6, 1944
18. a) Juno
19. c) Anthony McAuliffe
20. d) Reims